EMPOWERING THE TEEN YEARS

LIFE SKILLS FOR SUCCESS IN SCHOOL AND BEYOND

CLAUDE A. SMITH

QUICKENING PUBLISHING

CONTENTS

INTRODUCTION

Let's be honest, life is chaotic and messy, especially when you're a teenager. You have all sorts of stuff to worry about—like school, a social life, extracurricular activities, and sometimes work. Not only that, but the future is coming at you really fast. Soon you have to start thinking about things like how you're going to make money or what you want to do with your future. All of that is a lot to throw at someone who's not even an adult yet. Some people, however, seem better able to manage or roll with the punches than others. You may look at them and think, "I wish I had it all figured out," or even "What am I doing wrong?"

Well, you can take a deep breath. The problem isn't that you're necessarily doing anything wrong. What may be the case is that some people have better developed certain skills that can make life a little less chaotic. To put it simply: They have a better mastery of life skills.

"Life skills" is a term that isn't well defined. In short, life skills are a set of abilities and coping mechanisms that you need to live your life without letting the setbacks get you down. They can also be described as the practical application of certain skills that are required for a well-rounded life and a greater sense of resiliency (*Life Skills Education for Children and Adolescents in Schools*, 1994).

So far, it seems like common sense, right? In a way yes, a lot of life skills are simply using your best judgment. At the most basic level, life skills are essentially ways to make sure you get by as sane and healthy as possible—like how to take care of yourself and make sure all of your needs are met. But if it were really that easy, there would be no point in you reading past the first page! There are many reasons why some people might struggle with life skills. Often, it comes down to the fact that they simply were never taught these things.

For varying reasons, both parents and schools are often unequipped to teach life skills. In the case of schools, they often don't have adequate resources or funding to provide such additional education (Jenkins, 2022). At least half of parents also feel as though they are extremely unprepared or ill-equipped to take on the task (Richmond, 2021).

So, if your teachers and parents haven't been the ones keeping up with providing arguably the most fundamental skills for living, where does that leave you? To outline just how much this can affect one person versus another, we're going to compare Taryn's and Sally's stories.

Taryn was not taught life skills by his parents or at school. Now that he's 18, he doesn't know how to properly manage his schedule, eat healthy foods, handle anything involving banking, or plan out his budget. He lives in a constant state of stress and anxiety and is also experiencing a bunch of new health problems.

Sally, however, is succeeding in school by managing all her work, is already saving money for college, and has recently taken control of both her mental and physical health.

It definitely sounds like Sally has a much more firm grasp on life skills than Taryn. In fact, you could go so far as to say that Sally's overall sense of well-being and happiness is likely far greater than Taryn's.

Well, you picked up this book for a reason. We aren't promising that everything in here is going to make you a one-in-a-million success story just by following a few key guidelines; however, what we are hoping to achieve is to set you up for future success —not only in school but also further into your adult years.

To give you the best chance at success, we're going to leave you with a variety of different skills by the time you're ready to put this book down. The first thing we will tackle together is time-management skills, knowing how to schedule your time and manage deadlines and projects.

Next, we'll give you the tools to amp up your study skills. We hope that this segment of the book will prepare you for academic success, both in your current schooling and higher education. Not only that, but it can help you achieve academic goals and train you to be self-reliant and disciplined when it comes to taking control of your grades.

Communication is also an important part of life. Knowing how to properly formulate your thoughts and feelings will serve you well in your relationships, academic success, and future career in the workforce. Not only that, but you will be able to convey both how you feel and what you think in an articulate and easy-to-understand manner.

Of course, we can't forget that we live in a digital era. The internet is such a prevalent part of our modern lives that it's vital for you to learn skills for safe and responsible internet use. The internet has both positive and negative sides to it, and knowing how to properly navigate it is crucial for both your mental health and safety.

Finally, we'll demonstrate how the building blocks of a fully actualized life boil down to good mental and physical health. These are the building blocks to keeping your body and mind functioning and are the cornerstone of taking care of yourself and providing for your most basic needs.

But is all of this really necessary? At this point in your life, do you actually need to develop these skills to prepare for your future? We'll get into the more nuanced reasons why each subcategory of life skills is important the further along we get on this journey together. However, in the general sense, there are many benefits to taking a step forward and learning life skills. To be blunt: Life is full of stress. However, having the appropriate life skills to deal with stressful situations is kind of like wearing a coat when it's raining. You may still get wet but maybe not as bad. In other words, life skills allow you to deal with stress. They do so by equipping you with problem-solving skills and coping mechanisms (Parjapti et al. 2017).

We know life isn't easy. No one is going to hold your hand and lead you through life from cradle to grave. That doesn't mean you can't turn somewhere for help to get you started. We are here to help you solve some of the problems that life is going to keep throwing at you. The activities in this book will help you discover and practice proven strategies necessary for becoming a responsible young adult. Of course, you'll still have to put in the work. We're merely offering you guidance.

It's up to you to take charge and begin.

1

TIME-MANAGEMENT MASTER

Liam really has a lot on his plate. Just last week, he forgot about a homework assignment that was worth a good portion of his final grade, and he had to stay up all night to get it all done. Then, his basketball practice overlapped with his drum lessons. To add a cherry on top of the horrible week sundae, he promised to help his dad with yard work and had to cancel on a friend he forgot he made plans with. Meanwhile, he had all his usual responsibilities, such as other homework and household chores.

Seems like Liam has everything stacked really high on his plate. A slight puff of wind could probably send it all toppling down right on top of him. He barely seems like he's keeping it together because he is constantly forgetting things and double-booking himself. There are, however, things that Liam can do to help manage his schedule.

Keeping track of things is especially important in a school setting. Your teachers may tell you that things won't be super simple when you're in college or have a job, and you know what? They are sort of right about that! Let's look at academics. There is a direct correlation between appropriate time management and academic success. In fact, poor versus good time management can directly predict which students will achieve high or low grades (Arumugan et al., 2021).

Academic success isn't the only reason you should get good at time management. Proper time management has also been proven to reduce stress, give you a reputation for being reliable, keep you organized, and give you a better sense of focus on the tasks at hand (Arumugan et al., 2021). These are essential for virtually any stage of your life.

Time is money, after all, and we want to make good use of your purchase of this book. Let's begin!

SETTING PRIORITIES AND GOALS

Imagine for a moment that you took a nasty fall. You're bleeding pretty heavily from your arm, but you can also tell that you broke your ankle. Both hurt badly, and you definitely need to take care of something before help arrives. So, do you take care of the bleeding arm or the broken ankle? Realistically, as long as you don't move too much, the broken ankle can't possibly break any more than it already has. The bleeding, however, definitely needs more monitoring because blood loss will present a more imminent danger to your health.

Taking care of your responsibilities ideally isn't as dire as dealing with a medical emergency. However, it is important to figure out what requires your most immediate attention. You need to set priorities.

How do you set priorities? Well, one of the first steps to setting priorities is to consider what exactly you value (Tartakovsky, 2015). Do you value getting good grades? Do you value spending time with your friends and family? How much value do you put into these things when comparing them to each other? Asking yourself these questions helps you determine which tasks to put the most time and energy toward. However, consider what you value from an inward perspective rather than from external validation. After all, these priorities should benefit you first, as you're the one who's going to have to stick to them.

That's exactly why you should also consider what it is you want to make commitments to (Tartakovsky, 2015). Suppose your parents signed you up for saxophone lessons. The only problem is you hate playing the sax. In fact, you would rather do anything else. It becomes something you don't want to focus on or expend your energy toward. Rather, it becomes an empty priority.

Another way you can focus on your priorities is by setting goals. When you are working toward a goal, you have an achievement in mind. What your goal is directly affects how high you place it on your priority list.

Let's say you have two goals. One goal is to finish an art project by the end of the month. The other goal is to be able to sink more baskets in basketball by the end of the season. Since the art project would be due far earlier, you would prioritize this goal over your goal of improving your basketball skills.

It's also important that you reward yourself once you've completed your goals (Eastern Washington University, 2023). Think of it as triggering a bit of positive conditioning. When you reward yourself for your successes, you are more inclined to work toward that specific goal, as well as to reach other goals.

It's well and good enough to set goals, but do they actually work? Funnily enough, even the concept of setting a goal has been studied for its effectiveness. This is referred to as goal-setting theory as originally explored by Edwin A. Locke. In this theory, Locke suggested that setting concrete goals was more effective than merely hoping everything worked out in the end, as long as you "adopt a 'do-your-best' attitude" (Locke & Latham, 2002). Other research backs the effectiveness of setting goals as well. Researcher Emily VanSonneberg (2011) found in her case study that goals were directly tied to a feeling of overall happiness.

So, not only are goals a great way of getting things done, but they can also make you feel good when you accomplish them.

Break It Down

When you clean your room, you don't simply turn into a whirl-wind, throwing everything around and hoping that it lands in the right spot, do you? Of course not! You start with one small area and expand from there, or you break the cleaning into smaller tasks. It's the same when setting goals. You need to break them down.

One way you can break down goals is by accomplishing the more high-priority goals first. We touched base on that with our injury analogy at the beginning of the chapter, but let's look at it in a more precise manner. Let's say you have an assignment due on Tuesday and another one due on Friday. Obviously, you will want to put more of your focus on the assignment that is due sooner. If you neglect it for the later assignment, you're only going to wind up with rushed or sloppy work to present.

Another thing to help you further break down your goals is to make sure they are specific. After educator Emily VanSonnenberg assigned students an intention journal to write their goals in, she found the best results came from the students who set difficult yet specific goals (VanSonnenberg, 2011). So, if you have a goal to, say, get a better grade in biology, you wouldn't just say, "I want to do better in class." Rather, you could say, "I want to bring my grade up from a C to a B."

There is some evidence behind this, as "specific" also pertains to breaking down goals under the acronym SMART. When we're talking about setting SMART goals, what we mean is breaking down each goal into certain aspects to make them more attainable and easier to accomplish. To set a SMART goal, you need to make sure your goals are:

1. specific
2. measurable
3. attainable

4. relevant
5. time-based

So what do these points mean? "Specific" means that you need to really get to know what your goals are. In other words, what exactly is it that you want to achieve? Do you want better grades? Do you want to be more organized? Do you want to run faster? Find a way to name your goal so you know what it is you're working toward.

"Measurable" simply means that you can keep track of your progress. Let's say your goal is to run faster in gym class. You can measure your goal by timing yourself and keeping track of when you improve. If you want to earn more money, setting a certain amount is also a measurable goal.

It's well and good enough to shoot for your best, but your goals must also be attainable, or rather, "realistic." For example, it may be a stretch to assume that you can go viral and become the next big singer. However, it is more attainable to be able to increase your vocal range through practice.

"Time-based" is also pretty self-explanatory. Give yourself a deadline to achieve your goals. Let's say that you are saving up to buy your cousin something for Christmas. Nobody likes to shop too close to the holidays, so imagine that you set your goal for making the money by December 1.

Beyond being SMART, be sure to leave some room for flexibility when you set your goals as well. Not everything in life goes according to a 10-step plan. Sometimes, you have to be willing to shift the goalpost a little bit to accomplish a more realistic outcome than the one you originally set out to reach. You may also have to adjust deadlines because the one you gave yourself didn't work. Now, that doesn't mean being too soft on yourself when it comes to your goals. But if you don't allow for any breathing room at all, it's only a setup for disappointment and potential failure (Eastern Washington University, 2023).

Time-Block Techniques

Another means of accomplishing your tasks is to work within a time-blocking system. How time blocking works is that you take a period of time (such as a day) and divide the time further into "blocks" of time. For example, a block may be an hour, and each block, or hour, is devoted to a specific task (Griffin, 2021).

There are many different ways you can break down these blocks. While opinions on Elon Musk may be mixed, he has a technique for breaking down his daily schedule into five-minute blocks (Oshin, 2018). Of course, your goals and schedule are going to look a lot different as a teenager than a multi-billionaire CEO, and not everyone can handle having their schedule broken down quite as rigidly.

Instead, consider what you can accomplish in hour-long time blocks to start. Once you get the hang of it, you'll be able to break things down into smaller chunks.

Another way you can break tasks into a time block is through the Pomodoro Method (Cornell University, n.d.). The Pomodoro Method is a timed task completion method. To follow the Pomodoro Method, simply (Mandal, 2020):

1. Set a 25-minute timer.
2. Work for the 25 minutes without stopping.
3. When the timer goes off, stop working.
4. Take a timed break of 5 minutes.

While you'll want to be sure that you can take the occasional longer break here and there, this is a good method for getting you started in the mindset of scheduling out designated break times.

Prioritizing Tasks and Meeting Deadlines

You have a million things you need to get done this week. In fact, it seems like all you have are those dreaded deadlines looming over you like a threatening dark cloud. How do you figure out what you're supposed to do first? Which task is most important?

Do you notice that there is a certain time period in the day when you feel like you can get everything done? This would be your peak productivity period, and it differs for everyone. For some people, it might be that they start their day at their peak only to peter out as the afternoon wears on. For many others, they find that they can get the most accomplished in the late evening hours.

You can't realistically leave everything on your list for your peak productive period. However, what you *can* do is make the most of this time and get the most pressing things on your agenda done in that time period. In other words, this is the perfect time to tackle your high-priority tasks or to work on your most imminent deadline.

Another part of managing tasks is meeting deadlines. There's always something that needs to be accomplished by a deadline —whether it's homework or paying bills. Sometimes, though, they can be hard to keep track of. So how do you manage a deadline?

Taylor has a term paper of 10,000 words due at the end of the semester. Sounds like a very big project right? How can she make this deadline more manageable? Well, rather than focusing on the big deadline at the end of the term, she can break down the project into smaller deadlines (Filestage, 2018). Let's presume the semester is four months long. She can spend the first month organizing her topic and compiling her research. Then, she has until the end of the second month to create an outline. By the end of the third month, she has to meet half of the word count. In the homestretch of the final month, she finishes writing and editing her paper.

You also should be prepared for things to potentially get in the way of meeting your deadline, so always be ready for the potential of a setback. Pretend you have a project due and you suddenly lose three days of work because you had the flu. You need to be able to bounce back from all that time lost. What can help prevent this is making sure you give yourself enough time that you might be able to get ahead of the curve or maybe even complete a deadline early (Harper, 2023).

OVERCOMING PROCRASTINATION AND DISTRACTIONS

Aubrey has an assignment due at the end of the week. It's a reasonable timeframe for the project she has to complete. To complete it, she has to gather her research and then prepare for a classroom presentation. It seems straightforward and easy to do.

However, Aubrey seems to be having problems actually starting the project. Every time she tries to do her research, her mind wanders, and she finds herself surfing the internet on websites that have nothing to do with her project. Then, she decides that she's going to buckle down and do it. That is, as soon as she has completely reorganized her desk and her bedroom. Eventually, she forces herself to sit down and do it; but no matter how much she is screaming at herself to start the project, she just can't seem to make herself do it.

Perhaps you've been in a similar situation as Aubrey. If you have, what you're struggling with is likely procrastination. Procrastinating doesn't mean there's anything wrong with you, but it does make time management a lot harder.

However, there is often a root cause behind procrastination and, fortunately, there are many solutions.

What Is It That's Actually Stopping You?

A lot of people have the misconception that if someone has a problem with procrastination, then they are merely lazy (Butler, 2017). After all, if they can do it, you should be able to do it as well, right? Well, there is a lot of evidence that suggests that procrastination is not brought about by laziness. In fact, there are many common reasons why one might procrastinate.

When you think of a task you have to do, does the thought of doing it excite you? Chances are if the task is tedious or boring, you aren't going to be invested in it. Boredom can make tasks difficult to start because, quite frankly, all of our brains are kind of petulant like that. We crave exciting things and, honestly, if something doesn't fill us with joy or excitement, why would we bother with it (*The Real Reason You're Procrastinating*, 2022)?

There is also evidence to suggest that mental health may also play a role in causing procrastination. For example, procrastination can often be exhibited as a symptom by those who have attention deficit hyperactivity disorder (ADHD), regardless of whether they skew more toward either the inattentive or hyperactive spectrum of the disorder. Sometimes, the issue is that individuals with ADHD may have difficulty focusing on the task altogether; but at other times, the issue might be that they hyper-focus on tasks that may have nothing to do with the original task in the slightest (*The Real Reason You're Procrastinating* 2022).

Another reason why people who are diagnosed with ADHD can have problems with procrastination may very well be due to the phenomenon of time blindness (Trepany, 2023). Simply put, that means you have difficulty being able to tell how much time has gone by. In other words, when it comes to completing an assignment, a person with ADHD may not be able to guess how much time the task is actually going to take. So, let's pretend our friend Alice has ADHD. She may assume that the presentation assignment she has will take her only a single night to do, so she spends the rest of the week doing other things. When she finally discovers how much work the assignment is, she may realize too late that it will take her more than a single night's work.

Managing Distractions

Did you know that students in one study reported that when it came to doing homework, they felt distracted 37.8% of the time? That may not seem like a lot in the grand scheme of things, but if you think about it, it really adds up. This means that students are actually spending longer than necessary trying to do their homework because they feel more distracted than they would otherwise (Mrazek et al., 2021).

One of the biggest distractions you face may be in your pocket right now. Cellphones are practically pocket-sized computers capable of accessing the internet at any time. Unfortunately, that makes them a gateway for all kinds of distractions. Even just having your phone in the same room as you while you're working can make distraction all the more tempting (Mrazek et al., 2021).

So, how do you combat the allure of the digital world? To be rather blunt, you're going to have to put some kind of restriction on your phone usage. It's important that you are the one who upholds the restrictions instead of letting your parents do the hard work. When parents are the ones imposing some form of restricted phone use, many youths show reluctance about following the rules (Mrazek et al., 2021).

Keeping Focused

A big part of procrastination is an inability to focus on the task. That doesn't make sense! Concentrating on something should be the easiest task in the world, right? However, the task of concentrating is easier for some than others. As we've already touched on, people who particularly struggle with paying attention, such as those with ADHD and other neurodivergent conditions, may need to do things a little differently than their neurotypical peers.

One thing you can do to help focus if you have ADHD or trouble focusing is to work with a buddy. This "body-doubling" gives you a trusted person who can help keep you accountable and keep your focus on the task at hand. Not only that, but they can provide an example of a "calm and focused presence" and can also act as a motivator (ADDA Editorial Team, 2016).

There are more general things as well that can help you maintain focus. Taking short breaks can help reset your brain rather than forcing it to keep going for longer than it may be able to (Cherry, 2023). We can't keep focusing for an indefinite amount of time. Eventually, your brain is going to turn into soup if you try.

Under no circumstance should you attempt to multitask. As tempting as it is to try to get a million things done at once, all you're really doing is taking your focus and dividing it unnecessarily (Cherry, 2023). The brain only has so much holding power.

CREATING A BALANCED SCHEDULE AND SELF-CARE

No matter how much you feel like you have to hustle, you can't possibly do it all. Consider how your parents behave after they are at the end of a very long day. Whether they watch TV, read, or engage in some form of hobby, they are taking the time to unwind and get their minds off their day. In other words, even adults partake in self-care.

These days, there is a lot of emphasis on "hustling" and "grinding" to make the most out of our time and turn our time into profit.

How to Find the Balance

Not knowing where to draw the line between work and fun can lead to a lot of problems down the road. Think of it like you're staring at a beautiful buffet. On one side of it is all of your favorite snacks and junk food.

Finding a work-life balance is kind of like that. You can't just have fun all the time, because eventually, things begin to pile up. However, if you only worry about your responsibilities and commitments, your brain and body are going to turn into a pile of mush from overworking yourself.

But exactly how much time should you give to each part of your life? The field of psychology has come up with many ways to break down each part of your life. One of the most extreme ways is segmentation. This means that there is absolutely no overlap between your personal life and your work life in any way, shape, or form (Nortje, 2021). This is a rather extreme example of creating a work-life balance. As a teenager, it may not even be fully feasible for you. If we consider school the "work" aspect of your life, it can also bleed very heavily into the social part of your life as well.

Another thing you want to be mindful of is the spillover-crossover model. What this means is that essentially the things you do in your work and free time can influence the other areas of your life (Nortje, 2021). So, for example, if you spend all your time invested in your social life and hobbies, your school work can suffer. However, the same is true if you completely neglect the fun parts of your life for academic success.

However, that doesn't mean the spillover-crossover model is all negative. Sometimes positive occurrences in one area of life can benefit the other area as well (Nortje, 2021). So for instance, if you are well-rested and happy in your personal life, you are more likely to achieve academic success.

A good thing you can do to prevent the negative effects of this theory is to set clear boundaries. To do this, it's important to be assertive, yet polite (Nash, 2018). For example, let's say you are participating in the school play. Naturally, a lot of your time is going to be taken up rehearsing and getting ready for opening night. On top of that, you still have your studies and other commitments to take care of. Now, let's imagine one of your friends is asking for your time to help them out with a charity they are helping for extra credit. You could try to take it on top of your already packed schedule because you're a good friend and you want to help. However, you know it's just not feasible.

If you practice setting boundaries in this case, it can be as simple as:

"I'm really sorry. I would love to help out, but I actually have a lot going on right now. I'd love to make up for it and help out when my schedule is more open, if possible."

Let's look at a similar situation from the self-care side of things. You finally have a few moments to do something for yourself. However, your sibling knocks on your door and asks you to help them with their schoolwork. You still feel like you need a little more "you-time". What you can say in this case is:

"I'm taking some time for myself right now, but I would love to help you out later after I am well-rested."

As long as you remain respectful, other people should respect your boundaries as well. If they don't, are they really the type of person you want to devote so much time and energy to (Nash, 2018)?

Yes, You Need Self-Care

It can be very tempting to put away your needs for the sake of productivity. However, self-care is still a vital part of time management. You need to dedicate as much time to looking after yourself as you do to working hard.

There are many benefits to taking a little break here and there. Carving out time for self-care helps us manage and reduce our stress levels, as well as improve our overall sense of emotional well-being (Scott, 2020).

Self-care activities don't even have to be that complicated. You can start with very small moments for yourself. For example, you can treat yourself to a mini spa day by spending a little extra time on grooming, bathing, or even skincare (Scott, 2020). Pick out any activity that you can do just for yourself.

You may worry that taking time off to look after yourself is going to affect your productivity. But actually, it may be doing you more good than you realize.

Well-Being and Productivity

There is so much emphasis on hard work and going non-stop that people often forget that you physically can't keep going 24-7. You may think of your brain as this wrinkly lump of a computer firing productivity at all times. In reality, your brain has to take time and hit the "pause" button. If you don't do that, the "pause" button can become a big "stop" button. If you push too hard, all you're going to gain is the not-fun experience of burnout.

Sometimes, you simply need to take a step back and take a break. "But then I'm not getting any work done!" It does seem a little counterintuitive, doesn't it? But there is actually a method to the madness here. One study from the University of Waterloo found that when breaks were discouraged in the workplace, it had a direct negative effect on the productivity of employees (Consky, 2023).

Let's consider one of the most needed forms of self-care: sleep. It can be hard for some people to fully get the rest they need and maintain a good schedule for their circadian rhythm.

Sometimes, we even get tempted to forsake sleep to accomplish more. However, doing so may be harming your productivity rather than helping it.

For teenagers in particular, a good night's sleep directly results in better academic performance and concentration in school. The amount of sleep we get has a direct impact on our working memory (Capello, 2020). To fully get the benefits of a good night's sleep, adolescents aged 13–18 should be getting around 8–10 hours of sleep in a 24-hour period (Centers for Disease Control and Prevention, 2019).

REFLECTION

Now it's time to put what you've learned about time management into practice. To fully understand how to manage your time, we ask that you create and try to stick to a schedule. Think of everything you have to do during the week and write out specific times to accomplish each task. Make sure to plan out your time based on very specific things in your schedule. For example, set the high-priority tasks first. You can schedule everything from studying to snack breaks and after-school activities, such as sports, clubs, music lessons, etc.

It's important to have some means of keeping track of this schedule, too. One way you can do that is by using a planner. Not everyone likes planners; in fact, carrying one around all the time can be a bit of a pain. If you'd rather not have to physically write down your schedule, you can instead make use of a multitude of digital tools (MindTools Content Team, n.d.).

2

STUDY SKILLS

W e've all been there at one point: You're sitting at your desk, going over your notes and reading your text-book to prepare for an upcoming quiz. You roll your eyes as you flip the pages and wonder, "Why do I even need to study? I'd rather be doing anything else." Unfortunately, the answer is yes, you need to study, but you also need to know how to study.

How you study can make a vast difference in how well you do academically. However, it's not only about tackling it by reading your notes and textbook even more. Studying is kind of like preparing for a battle. In other words, to "win, "you need a strategy. A study from Stanford University found that strategic studying led to an increased score of one-third of a letter grade (Martinovich, 2017). Not only that, but proper test preparation can greatly reduce your risk of experiencing some form of test anxiety (Yusefzadeh et al., 2019). All the best strategies also rely on using a variety of different skills. Knowing a variety of study skills has been directly linked to qualitative academic achievements.

ACTIVE READING AND NOTE-TAKING STRATEGIES

Have you ever been certain that you have all the information you learned in class completely memorized, only to struggle to remember it when it counts, like during an exam? Part of the problem could be in how well you actually understand the material. The two key components of memorizing and revising are active reading and how you take notes in class.

Active Reading and Better Reading Comprehension

When you read something, are you actually absorbing and comprehending the words in front of you? Let's ask you this: Are you *actively* reading it? Simply put, active reading means not just merely reading the words in front of you, but understanding and engaging with the text as well (*Critical Reading Techniques*, 2018).

You can start by making note of the main thesis or point of the text, that is, what is it saying or trying to accomplish? This gives you a place to begin, which makes the rest of the reading easier to digest. After each chapter, it can help to create your own summary. Note any key points or events from each segment, such as who was involved and what happened (*Active Reading Strategies*, n.d.).

But if you really want to engage with a text, you need to do more than simply summarize what happened. Many texts contain so much information and varying ideas that it can be hard to keep track of everything. Some methods that can help in this case are to create your own annotations or create mind maps, flow charts, or diagrams that can help link ideas that share a similar theme (*Active Reading Strategies*, n.d.).

Another way to improve your reading comprehension is by expanding your vocabulary (Rosenkrantz, 2022). Now, you don't need to go crazy with it. The key to increasing your vocabulary is incorporating it into everyday life. You're not likely to use a word like "sesquipedalian" in your everyday vocabulary. However, there are other things you can do, like write down new and interesting words and their meanings or engage with a variety of literature and media (Piontec, 2020).

Have you ever noticed in English class that your teacher will often have you and your classmates take turns reading and discussing the reading material? This is a concept known as reciprocal teaching, and it is an effective strategy for increasing reading comprehension (Rosenkrantz, 2022). You can even make it fun by creating your own mini book club or study group with friends.

Note-Taking Strategies

How do you take notes when you're in class? You might say, "What do you mean, how do I take notes? I just have to write down what the teacher says or whatever they put up on the board." If that's your answer, you may be surprised to find that you aren't taking notes efficiently at all.

There is a lot more to taking notes than simply jotting down the information. There are many different strategies that have been developed for note-taking. Cornell University developed its own method of note-taking, known simply as the Cornell Method (*Guides: Study Effectively*, 2017). To follow the Cornell Method, you need to divide your note-taking paper into three parts. The first and largest part should be on the right-hand side of the paper. This is the segment where you will write down the information presented by your teacher, both verbally and written. On the left-hand side in the margin, you are going to place any questions or "cues" you have about the material. Finally, the bottom portion of the page is dedicated to summarizing the notes (*Guides: Study Effectively*, 2017).

You can also organize your notes into a more chart-like format as well. The charting method of notetaking works by dividing the information into both categories and subcategories in a chart-like format akin to a spreadsheet. This method is really effective at keeping your notes concise and allowing you to memorize topics by drawing connections between them. However, one potential drawback of the charting method is that you need to be able to identify and keep the subcategories well organized for them to make sense when you read them later science-related. It is also not easily applicable to fast-paced or technical classes. For example, you may struggle to use it in a science-related class as opposed to something like English or history (Moffatt, n.d.).

Annotations and Highlighting

When you are reading something like a textbook or even a book from your English class, do you have a system to mark important segments to refer back to later? If not, consider either annotating or highlighting the text.

Using a highlighter pen can be a useful tool for remembering information. However, it is important to remember that sometimes less is more. The main issue of highlighting is that many students will often go a little overboard and highlight almost everything. In reality, you really only need to highlight specific information to get the most out of this method. What you should focus on when highlighting is the integral information (*Highlighting*, 2016). Say you wanted to highlight important stuff in your history textbook or notes about the Prohibition era. Instead of highlighting every little thing about the time period, you could highlight information such as important dates, events, or people.

It's also important that you really curb that temptation to make the text a thick block of neon yellow. In this case, covering more information isn't going to do you much good in the long run. Consider highlighting only a handful of words per paragraph and make sure those words relate back to the key concepts we just mentioned (*Highlighting*, 2016).

Annotating, on the other hand, refers to any marking to the text that's made to help you remember information, as well as to gain a further understanding of the text. So, the highlighting we talked about is really just another form of annotating the text. However, it can also involve writing in the margins, underlining, and circling information. You can use a variety of annotations to keep track of certain information. However, that can get a little messy if you don't organize it properly. One tip that might keep you from getting mixed up with your annotations is to create a legend. This way, you can keep track of things such as what information you're trying to remember with each specific annotation. You can also use a variety of symbols to keep track of certain areas. For example, if you are uncertain about a segment, you could use a question mark (Pfleegor, 2021).

MEMORY TECHNIQUES AND STUDY HABITS

Has this ever happened to you? You studied hard and long for a big test. Then, your teacher puts the paper down on the desk, and all of a sudden... poof. Everything you reviewed is suddenly just gone. You know you studied. You put in an immense amount of work for weeks to prepare. So, why can't you remember the material?

Everyone has been in that boat at least once in school. When you consider all the stuff you have to cram in there between your different classes—not to mention other information bombarding you outside the classroom—is it any wonder some information can slip your mind? It's particularly frustrating when you need that information during the test.

What if the problem isn't you but the way you're studying? It may shock you, but there is a smart way to study and a wrong way to study.

Mnemonics and Memory Aids

It's one thing to read your textbooks and take notes. But all of that is useless if you can't remember any of the study material once it's test time. Our brains are really good at remembering things, as long as you give them the right tools.

Mnemonics are things that trigger your brain to remember certain information. There are many different types of mnemonics. One of the most common and popular types of mnemonic devices are acronyms (Pederson, 2016). So, let's say you are trying to remember how to operate a device. A key component to operate this device is to turn on the lever to the left. You could remember it with the acronym TOLL. This could stand for Turn On Left Lever.

Think of your favorite song for a moment. Can you recite all the lyrics? Our brains are really adept at memorizing things when they are set to a catchy tune (Pederson, 2016). If you're struggling to remember some information, consider setting it to the background of a song and see if that helps.

There are other things you can do besides using certain mnemonics. For example, when you write out your notes, you are also engaging in an activity that can help you with memory recall.

There is also some evidence that the five senses can be engaged in triggering our memories as well (Ernst et al., 2021). However, recalling information through your senses during a test can be a bit tricky. One way you could use this hack is by using the gum trick. When you are studying, chew a particular flavor of gum. Every single time you study or do homework, only chew on that flavor. Or conversely, you could wear a specific perfume, cologne, or scent to get the same effect.

The Perfect Study Environment

Do you think you could prepare for an exam at a music concert? How about in a gym full of people watching a basketball game? We assume that your answer is, "No, of course not! How can anyone concentrate in that environment?" Where we study has just as much of an effect on our ability to concentrate and retain information as other factors of good study habits.

Creating an environment that's perfect for studying is very simple. The first thing you have to do is make sure that your environment is free from distractions (*How to Create a Study Space*, 2020). When you're studying for an exam and your sibling walks into the room, it throws you off your groove, right? That's why it's important to significantly reduce distractions.

While limiting distractions—particularly distracting noises—is important for an academic environment, it's also true that certain background noise can be of great benefit to you. In one study, they found that background music greatly increased memory capacity (Lehmann & Seufert, 2017).

Now, think about how the space feels. Do you like the chair you're sitting in? Is it just right or is it kind of hard and annoying to sit on for a long period of time? You want your study space to be completely comfortable (*How to Create a Study Space*, 2020) After all, as a student, you'll be spending a lot of time in there. But you also don't want it to be too comfortable. Studying on your bed, for example, isn't ideal. Not only does it affect your ability to focus or be productive, but it can also negatively impact your ability to sleep (Hubbard, 2020).

A good part of how to make the space feel right is the lighting. You want the lights to be just right to get in the mood for studying (*How to Create a Study Space*, 2020). During the daytime, natural lighting can have great benefits on your mood and your ability to concentrate. In fact, one study found that natural lighting was the most effective for engaging productivity and academic performance in students (Shishegar & Boubekri, 2016). However, you also don't want the light to affect the visibility of any computer screen you may be using, as that would be even more counterintuitive (*How to Create a Study Space*, 2020).

When you study, do you scatter all your notes and supplies across the table or your desk? It's important to keep your study environment clean and well-organized (*How to Create a Study Space*, 2020). Clutter can be very negative in creating a calm and positive study environment. A messy environment causes issues such as stress and can even impair your memory (Brody, 2021). Keep your work area clear and you won't experience the hassle of fumbling around for notes, pens, or anything else you may need while you're studying.

Exam Preparation and Test-Taking

Now, you have your perfect study area ready to go, and you're armed with a list of different memory aids. Time to knuckle down and study. Remember how we mentioned that there are more effective ways to study than others? What it all comes down to is whether you engage in good study habits or bad ones.

To begin with, you need to get in the right mindset about studying. You know how when you like the subject you're taking, studying for the tests feels a lot easier? There's a reason for that. Approaching studying with a positive mindset can greatly affect your ability to tackle the material, especially if it seems difficult or challenging (Lovering, 2022).

You don't only want to look at your text and re-read the same information you already covered in class. Use different tools and strategies. You can review what you know by quizzing yourself. An effective way of doing that might be through using flashcards as a tool. Even our previously mentioned note-taking strategies and mnemonic devices can be effective for the purpose of reviewing (Lovering, 2022).

However, not everyone studies the same way. For example, do you find that you have a hard time keeping yourself on task and motivated when you study alone? You can counteract this by forming a study group with your peers. Studying with friends can greatly increase your chances of success. One study found that students at risk of college-level failing a college-level course fared far better when engaging in group studying than when they studied solo (Thalluri, 2016).

One thing you absolutely want to avoid is cramming. It is tempting, especially if you wound up procrastinating for whatever reason. However, it simply doesn't work. In fact, it may be doing you a lot more harm than good. Think about it: You're basically trying to force a bunch of things on your short-term memory, as opposed to your long-term memory (Lane, 2020).

Not only that, but you're also more likely to get really stressed out before and during your exam (Lane, 2020).

This especially applies to late-night cramming. Sometimes, you're going to want to spend all night studying to make sure you understand everything and are ready for test day. Resist that urge with all of your might! The last thing you want is to be falling asleep right in the middle of an important exam. A good night's sleep is crucial for doing well on any test. The reason for this is that being well-rested has direct benefits on memory recall, as opposed to when you're tired (Capello, 2020).

So, you've studied and are certain that you've prepared sufficiently for the exam. It's now time to talk about actually taking the test. All you have to do is sit down and answer the questions to the best of your abilities, right? Well, what if we were to tell you that there is a right way and a wrong way to take an exam?

Let's start by having you ask yourself a question. When you're getting ready to take an exam, does your stomach churn at the mere thought of it? Do you feel sweaty and jittery, just like a big bundle of nerves? What you are experiencing is test anxiety (Hoffses, 2018). The good news is that test anxiety is ridiculously common. However, the bad news is that test anxiety can greatly inhibit your exam performance (Yusefzadeh et al., 2019).

But you don't have to let test anxiety get the best of you. Fortunately, some of the preparation tips we've already covered are exactly what you need to beat this! When you use the right study tools to encourage preparation long before the exam, you'll feel less anxiety when you take the test (Hoffses, 2018).

Sometimes, though, there is nothing you can do but ask for help—especially when your test anxiety is a major hindrance. See if your school offers any sort of accommodations or assistance that might help alleviate your test anxiety by speaking to your teacher or a counselor (Hoffses, 2018).

Alright, let's set those nerves aside and get to the test-taking. How you go through the test itself can increase your chances of success. The first step is keeping a positive mindset. Now, considering we just talked about test anxiety, this is easier said than done. But if you go in with a negative mindset, you are definitely going to psych yourself out.

Skim through the test before answering any questions. Not only will this give you a good idea of what's on the test, but you can also properly judge the length of the test and get an estimate of how long it should take you. Say, for example, you have a test with short-answer and long-answer questions. After reading over the test, you may decide that the best strategy is to start with the short questions before dedicating yourself to the long-form questions.

Honestly, it doesn't matter what order you answer questions on a test. You might be tempted to time-consuming try and buckle down on a particularly challenging question until you get it right. However, that can be counterintuitive and time-consuming. It's better to skip questions you aren't sure about and come back to them later.

Finally, don't obsess over the clock. If you're running out of time, don't let that freak you out! The important thing is that you are doing your best to complete the test. This doesn't mean you have to answer every question. If on the opposite side of the coin, however, you find that you have time left over, use it to your advantage and review, review, review (O'Shea, 2023).

CRITICAL THINKING AND PROBLEM-SOLVING

Life is constantly going to throw problems at you. In school, a lot of your problems can be solved by using critical thinking and problem-solving skills. You use these skills outside the classroom as well—more than you probably realize!

When we use our problem-solving skills, it shows our capability to handle unexpected or complex situations. This even includes making simple decisions like the ones you make on a daily basis (Indeed Editorial team, 2023b)

Developing critical thinking comes with its own challenges. Often, we tend to rely on our gut feelings or what we can observe at face value (Smaltz, et al., 2017). But as you begin to develop these tools over time, you'll find a whole world of new information you didn't even know was right in front of you.

Developing Analytical and Critical-Thinking Skills

Analytic and critical-thinking skills are both vital aspects of problem-solving. With analytical skills, you need to be able to take in information to identify a problem, observe the facts, and create your own conclusion. Analytical skills are particularly useful for really complex problems (Indeed Editorial Team, 2021).

Critical thinking is equally important. It can give you the tools to make informed decisions and create your own opinions on matters, and it can increase your curiosity and problem-solving skills (*The Benefits of Critical Thinking for Students*, 2021).

One of the first ways to become more analytical is to increase your knowledge in general. You don't even have to do this part in school! There are many different ways you can increase your knowledge. Consume a wide variety of educational material (Indeed Editorial Team, 2021). This can be anything from books and documentaries to presentations, podcasts, and more.

For some, a bunch of numbers can be very confusing. This makes learning how to read data seem like a major roadblock. However, data literacy is vital for learning how to think analytically. Trends in data can show us a variety of information and trends in information as well. If you have difficulty with data, some things you can do are practice with mock data sheets or see if there are any free analytics courses near you (Cote, 2021).

Developing analytical skills doesn't have to be all work and no play. You can engage your brain in an analytical sense in many fun ways. For instance, if you are really good with numbers or are looking to be better with them, you could consider doing sudoku puzzles. Ever play a game of Clue? Anything involving mystery-solving is also a great way to practice analyzing minute details (Indeed Editorial Team, 2021).

You also have to be able to distinguish and analyze opposing viewpoints. While this can be used to compare data in a numerical sense, there are other applications of this idea as well (Cote, 2021). If one of your friends likes pineapple on their pizza but the other doesn't, neither of them is technically wrong. However, you can take both of their viewpoints, consider them, and decide for yourself if you also like pineapple on pizza.

Similarly to checking out other viewpoints, it's also important for critical thinking that you continue to question things (*The Benefits of Critical Thinking for Students*, 2021). The correct answer to any question is never simply "because things are the way they are." When you ask the who, the what, the where, and the why, you aren't always going to get a satisfying answer, but you'll grow your scope of knowledge. Not only that but you'll be better equipped for problem-solving. It's only through asking questions that you can reach a sense of clarity and understanding about a problem and, therefore, be more able to solve it (Birt, 2023).

Similarly, you also need to evaluate any evidence that you come across. We'll get a bit more into how to do this later when it comes to determining whether information is presented as factual. However, it can also give you a baseline to work off a problem by examining your past experiences (Birt, 2023).

Problem-Solving Strategies

Let's start at the beginning. To solve a problem, the first step you have to take is to analyze it. There are many different methods that you can use to analyze virtually any problem. It all boils down to what exactly the problem is.

Some problems can be solved with the Kipling method, otherwise known as the 5W method. To use the Kipling method, you simply have to ask a few questions meant to make the problem clearer. These questions are, "Who, what, when, where, and why?" (Muscad, 2022). Say you're reading a book for English class and the teacher asks you to talk about the central conflict of the story. You can use the Kipling method to solve this problem by asking something along the lines of:

1. Who is causing the conflict?
2. What is the conflict about?
3. When does the conflict take place in the novel?
4. Where does the conflict occur?
5. Why is the conflict happening?

Asking yourself these questions gives you a much deeper understanding of the text than if your answer was simply, "The main character is clashing with the antagonist." With these questions, you can get to the real heart of the story, like why the protagonist and antagonist aren't getting along, or what led to them fighting in the first place. It's the same when you apply this method to any problem. Once you start asking yourself these questions and relating them back to the "problem," you can get to the root of the issue and solve it.

You've analyzed the nature of the problem. Now, we have to get into the matter of creating a resolution. One of the first things you may be tempted to do is the tried-and-true method of brainstorming (Waters, 2022). Brainstorming is an effective strategy for coming up with a solution, especially if it requires working with other people or needing to use a dose of creativity (MindTools Content Team, 2023).

Heuristics is another method of problem-solving that you can employ. Heuristics is particularly good for taking complex problems and breaking them down into something more solvable. However, the downside to heuristics is that it's essentially a "mental shortcut" designed to give our brains the quickest means of reaching a solution (Chen, 2022).

What that means is that heuristics can employ several different methods. One such method is through confirmation bias. If you truly believe something to be true and something seems to confirm it, you're only going to double down on this. Another type of bias that employs heuristics is hindsight bias or, rather, because something already happened, it's very likely to happen again (Chen, 2022). As you can see, although it can lead to many quick solutions, there are many pitfalls to this particular type of problem-solving.

You can also work on your skills that are essential to problem-solving. You will face many different problems, academically and otherwise. Therefore, it's important to build upon your skills to give you the best chance at tackling any problem in a well-rounded manner. Some examples of skills you can take the time to develop include leadership, communication, analyzing data and research, people skills, and more (Waters, 2022). If some of that sounds familiar, you can rest easy knowing that this book is going to equip you with these skills.

Applying Logic and Reasoning

You can't solve any problems without the use of logic and reasoning. When you have a problem and you want to solve it with logic, there are many steps to how you have to look at the problem.

So, let's say you are trying to solve a problem about how to fix a door frame. The first step is to collect all the information that you know. For example, how is the door broken? For the sake of argument, let's assume the hinge is loose. Then, you need to analyze the information that you have. How badly is the hinge loosened? Do you have the right tools to fix it? Finally, you need to form a conclusion (*How Logical Reasoning Works*, n.d.). After carefully looking over the problem of the door hinge, you conclude that all it needs is a little bit of tightening with a Phillips screwdriver.

But beyond that, you also have to support your conclusion (*How Logical Reasoning Works*, n.d.). Say your dad is arguing with you about how to fix the door. You can explain what information you have analyzed to tell him how the hinge came loose and even show him the shape of the screw to support your choice of tools. Then, you have to defend your conclusion, which you would do by physically showing him that the screw fits the nail.

It may come as a surprise, but there are many different kinds of logical reasoning we use regularly. Sometimes, we can even use logic and reasoning for fun. One study found that when playing the video game World of Warcraft, the players consistently had to problem-solve and utilize their resources to get the best performance out of their characters, as well as to overcome obstacles (Emihovich et al., 2020).

REFLECTION

Consistency with studying has been proven to be the key. One way that you can put this into practice is by creating a study schedule. Consider what you need to study and devote a specific amount of time solely for the purpose of studying. To be even more effective, try breaking down the schedule time-blocking further by subjects being studied (*How to Make an Effective Study Plan*, n.d.). It's a great means of practicing that time-blocking technique we talked about in the previous chapters!

Speaking of burning out, make sure to schedule breaks. You also have to factor in non-study-related tasks for studying, such as eating, extracurriculars, chores, relaxation time, etc. (*Guidelines for Creating a Study Schedule*, n.d.).

Remember that even though you are setting up a study routine, it's important to allow for a little bit of flexibility to adjust your studying time and length. No week is ever going to replay the exact same way. Things always come up, and you're going to need to roll with each bump in the road from time to time.

3

COMMUNICATION

People often thought that Skylar was shy. She never really seemed to say much to anyone. The problem, however, wasn't that Skylar didn't have anything to say. In fact, she had a lot to say. She had strong opinions and witty comments she knew would make other people laugh. No matter how hard she tried, though, she struggled to express herself.

But that didn't stop her from wanting to improve. Skylar would stand in front of a mirror for hours and practice what she was going to say. Whenever she had to do a presentation, she wrote and rewrote her talking points until they flowed beautifully. Soon, she was engaging more in class. Finally, she overcame her stage fright and even joined the school debate team!

Unless you take a complete vow of silence or decide to live as a hermit, you're going to need to know how to communicate with other people. Good communication skills are vital when it comes to interacting with others. For starters, good communication eliminates misunderstandings and reduces conflict because it encourages people to openly discuss things in a constructive manner. It also builds trust between others and makes it easier to form a relationship with them (*The 7 Benefits of Effective Communication*, 2019). This can benefit you in virtually all areas of your life.

However, there is so much nuance in communication. If you don't know what you're doing, many things can get lost in translation—especially when you factor in nonverbal communication. You need to know how to speak, observe, and listen if you want to make sure that you truly understand somebody.

So let's talk.

VERBAL COMMUNICATION AND PUBLIC SPEAKING

Harper has to present a speech at her school assembly. The very thought of it makes her stomach twist. Her throat goes dry as she walks up to the podium, and the words fall silent on her tongue.

Unless you plan on only communicating nonverbally for the rest of your life, you're going to have to get used to talking to people. Verbal communication is the foundation of almost everything that makes us human. Communication is connection, and so much of life is about connecting with other people.

Sometimes, you'll have to take your communication skills to an even bigger audience. Does the idea of speaking in front of a large group of people make you break out in hives? Glossophobia, or the fear of public speaking, is actually a quite common phobia (Black, 2017). However, that doesn't undercut its necessity. Imagine that years down the line, you're working in sales for a company. You'd have to get pretty used to public speaking just to be able to do your job and pitch your brand or product to potential clients. Virtually any career can benefit from public speaking skills, and they help improve your professional reputation. Public speaking also encourages networking and forming connections with others (Carlton, 2021).

Talking to other people can be intimidating. We don't always know the right thing to say or how to even say it in a way that gets our point across. But, with the right set of communication skills, you can finally speak your mind.

Be Clear and Confident

Tell us what scenario sounds better: Tanner and Ryan are both trying to talk to their teacher about their recent grades. Ryan fumbles with his words and doesn't come across as very confident in his defense of his argument. Tanner, however, approaches the teacher very clearly and confidently, respectfully explaining the situation and asking how he can improve. If you said Tanner probably had more success, you would be correct!

Being clear and confident is crucial to communication skills. For one thing, being clear about what you are asking eliminates the chance of something getting lost in translation. Confidence can also help your case. Imagine for a moment that you are giving a presentation on the life cycle of the monarch butterfly. If you lack confidence in your presentation, then no one is going to think you know what you're talking about—even if your presentation of the facts is entirely accurate. You'll also likely be less nervous when you have to speak in front of a large group of people if you have the confidence to back yourself up.

Another thing that can help you is practicing what you're going to say well in advance. While something like a conversation is a little unpredictable compared to, let's say, a presentation, it still doesn't hurt to practice your opener.

First, let's examine the technical aspects of verbal communication. Part of speaking clearly is making sure that you are easy to understand. The most important way to do this is to enunciate each word that falls off your tongue.

The best exercise you can do to practice enunciation is tongue twisters (Edgar, 2022). If you've ever heard the Peter Piper rhyme, that's an excellent example of a tongue twister. If none of the classic ones are to your taste, try inventing your own and get really creative with it. For example:

"Polly Pocket packed pretty purses."

It may seem a bit silly at first, but once you get the hang of it, tongue twisters can really help with overcoming certain words and making sure you are pronouncing things clearly.

Another way you can help your enunciation is by recording yourself speaking. Take note of any words you may be slurring, stuttering, or mumbling, among other minor slips. You can use your recordings as a reference to continuously practice and improve, (Edgar, 2022).

Tone can also make or break communication. In some cases, if your tone is too emotional, it may have the opposite effect than the outcome you are hoping for. It is true that a passionate tone can be moving, however, you don't want to come across as so emotional that you completely negate the need for logic and reason either (Brower, 2023).

When it comes to communicating confidently, you also want to keep in mind to temper your confidence to avoid sounding like a stuck-up know-it-all. No one enjoys talking to someone who seems arrogant (Brower, 2023). It might also be helpful to avoid or limit the use of sarcasm.

Overcome Stage Fright and Perform Flawless Presentation

You may feel embarrassed if you get shy at the idea of speaking. However, many noteworthy people have also had similar anxieties regarding communication. The good news is that because so many others have experienced some form of stage fright, there are plenty of ways to overcome it.

Think of public speaking the same as performing in a play. Even seasoned actors have a tendency to get nervous before performing in front of hundreds of people multiple times in a row. So, how do actors shake out their nerves before literally speaking for a living? Well, they have exercises that prepare them before they go on stage.

One exercise in particular that might help you with stage fright is to quite literally shake it out. Moving your body will help shake out any physical tension lingering in your body. In a similar vein, imagine that you are holding a ball of energy. Get a feel for how big it is and how it feels, then throw it away to release the built-up energy (Backstage Staff, 2022).

You can also do vocal exercises to prepare your voice. Get yourself in the right mindset by practicing your articulation and enunciation out loud. You can do this with a presentation by speaking it out loud. Notice any areas where you may be coming across unclear. Another way you can practice your diction is through tongue twisters (Backstage Staff, 2022).

There are also some general tips and tricks that can help you overcome the feelings of stage fright. Neither is inherently better than the other. It really boils down to what works best for you. For example, if you find yourself getting overwhelmed by the sheer size of the audience, it can be helpful to focus on one person. It doesn't matter who you choose to focus your gaze on, as long as they feel familiar and comfortable to you (*Got Stage Fright?*, 2022). For example, if you see someone with a similar haircut to a friend, you could imagine that you're looking at them in the audience instead of a total stranger.

Got some of that nervous energy out? Good to hear! Now comes the hard part: actually getting on stage and rocking everyone with a fantastic presentation. But it's not enough to just stand up there and deliver the words monotonously.

Who is it that you are trying to reach with your words? When giving a presentation, it's important to know your audience. For instance, if you're trying to give a speech to your fellow students, you aren't going for the same kind of delivery you would if you were reciting a eulogy at a funeral or a Shakespearian monologue. You want your dialogue to contain enough professionalism to impress your teachers, but you still don't want to bore your classmates to death by being too technical. The same would go for a business proposal. You wouldn't engage with someone in the workplace the same way you would if you were speaking to only your friends.

Above all, the best way to overcome your nerves is to make sure your presentation is well-prepared (*How to Improve Your Presentation Skills*, 2022). After all, if you know your presentation is flawless, you have nothing to worry about. Humor us for a moment. If you have any kind of inanimate object lying around your room, pick it up and put it on your bed. Now, imagine that this object is a person. Practice your presentation in front of it. When you get comfortable with that, move on to asking your family or friends to be the audience for your presentations. If you anticipate the possibility of a Q&A segment during or after the presentation, encourage your practice audience to ask questions. They may give you insight into what to prepare for. That way, you aren't blindsided by a question you may not have otherwise been expecting.

Active Listening and Empathetic Communication

So far, we have been focusing on the speaking aspect of communication. However, there is more to communication than learning how to get your point across. A crucial part of effective communication is listening to the other party as well. Seems pretty straightforward so far, right? But there is more to listening than simply hearing the words that come out of another person's mouth.

By that, we mean that the skill you need to practice is active listening. What "active listening" means is that you make an effort in a conversation, not only to hear the other side of it but to also come to an understanding of the other person, as well as the meaning and intent behind their words.

The first part of active listening is to ensure that you are engaged fully in the conversation. Pay attention to everything the other party is saying.

How you respond to what they say can also show that you are listening attentively. You can showcase this by asking for clarity. For example, "What I'm hearing you say is..." You can also encourage them to elaborate or continue expressing themselves by asking questions (Cuncic, 2022).

To give you a further understanding of active listening, here is an example:

Yasmin: "I just feel really stressed lately."

Jay: "I'm sorry to hear that you've been feeling this way. Do you want to talk about it?"

Yasmin: "There's just so much on my plate! My boss asked me to take an extra shift, and we have that test coming up Friday. What if he says no?"

Jay: "What I'm hearing is you might be worried about your boss being angry with you. Why do you think that?"

Another skill important for communication is empathy. There are three types of empathy that are fundamental to communication. Those types are compassionate, cognitive, and emotional empathy there are. Confused that there are so many different types of empathy? It's pretty easy to explain. In this scenario, your friend Meg has come to you feeling upset that her cat has died. Compassionate empathy is basically taking your empathy and responding to it with an action (Clarke, 2019). If your friend were to come to you and say that their pet had died, a way you can respond that would echo compassionate empathy might be, "I'm really sorry to hear that. Please let me know if there's anything I can do to help you during this difficult time."

In the case of cognitive empathy, you would imagine what it would be like to lose your own pet. Cognitive empathy is essentially when you "walk a mile in someone else's shoes" (Clarke, 2019). When you do that, you get a pretty good idea of how Meg is feeling. If you were using emotional empathy, seeing Meg so distraught would be enough to cause you a great deal of distress. You'd probably be crying right alongside her.

By engaging your empathy when listening to other people, you are letting them know that you are someone they can feel safe around. You create a space in which they and their feelings or concerns matter. This will encourage communication between the both of you on a deep level.

WRITTEN COMMUNICATION AND EFFECTIVE WRITING

You ever wonder why your English teacher is so passionate about teaching you certain books and assigning you short stories and essays? To some, the idea of writing seems utterly useless. But there is great power in written communication. From a future career perspective, a good number of jobs require some degree of written communication for you to be successful (Indeed Editorial Team, 2023).

How to Write an Essay

The essay is either your favorite type of assignment or the one you dread the most. By this point in your school years, you've probably written at least one essay, or are just getting into the mechanics of how essay writing works.

The essay consists of several different parts. Naturally, your introductory paragraph is the first. This is where you present your topic and your argument. A topic, for example, might look like: "The Use of Biodegradable Plastic Alternatives." Your argument, however, might be that "biodegradable plastic alternatives benefit the environment in the long term."

Next come the body paragraphs. This is where you outline all the evidence for your argument. Each of your body paragraphs should introduce an idea applicable to your argument, as well as outline evidence supporting the topic. So, if we were going on the biodegradable plastics topic, each paragraph could be talking about the pros and cons of different plastic alternatives.

To support your argument in each body paragraph, you need appropriate evidence to back it up. Primary and secondary sources are the lifeblood of the essay. Without them, you could claim something completely outlandish like "biodegradable plastics are a conspiracy theory designed to shut down oil companies."

Finally, you have your conclusion. This is where you wrap your entire essay into a nice little bow. In other words, what is the resulting point of your arguments or findings? Is there anything that could be researched further, and what is the big picture of your essay? For example, is there a long-term benefit to biodegradable plastic? What are the implications of using biodegradable plastics? Are there any cons to using them, or does more research need to be done to understand their limitations?

There are many technical aspects that also make or break your essay. How well does each paragraph flow into the next? Is your evidence relevant to the topic? Even spelling and grammar play important parts in whether or not your essay can really shine (Medojevic, 2022).

Even the voice you use when writing can make a difference. Your writing is a lot stronger when you use active voice as opposed to passive voice (Indeed Editorial Team, 2023a). But what distinguishes active from passive writing? Let's look at two different sentences:

Passive: "I have gone to the store."

Active: "I went to the store."

See how that's not only more concise but more dynamic as well? You want the words to get to the point and punch across the page.

Power of Persuasion

You don't just want to spew a bunch of malarkey with your writing. If all you wanted to do was jot some random words on paper, you wouldn't get very far. You want to convey a message or some meaning with your writing. You also want your reader to see your perspective and maybe even get them to reconsider their own perspective. To do that, you need your writing to be persuasive.

What is the key to being persuasive? It all comes down to appealing to an audience, even when readers. There are three means of appealing to your readers in a persuasive essay: ethos, logos, and pathos. To elaborate, when you want to persuade someone, you need to use a good balance of logic (logos), pathos (emotion), and ethics (ethos) (*Pathos, Logos, and Ethos,* 2021).

Let's break this down further. Your English teacher assigns you a persuasive essay based on whether or not the school should consider the use of standardized student uniforms. You get your argument all laid out, but now you need to convince them of your stance on uniforms. If you were to approach this logically, your essay will outline the pros and cons of the uniforms. Ethically, if you were arguing against the introduction of uniforms, you could outline an argument on how enforcing such a dress code infringes upon the rights of your fellow students. Even right there where you are appealing to ethics, you are also appealing to the emotions that may be enough to persuade the school administration against taking such a drastic step. By highlighting a sense of injustice toward your peers, you're appealing to sympathy.

Tweak That First Draft?

Have you ever handed in an essay only to be greeted with a bunch of red ink outlining spelling or grammar mistakes, even though you were almost certain that your writing was flawless? Editing and proofreading are essential to good writing. Let's ask a simple question: Did you hand in the first draft?

That is a big mistake a lot of people make when it comes to writing. The only way to avoid it is by doing arguably the most dreaded part of writing. After you finish the first draft of any essay, the next step is to proofread and edit the paper.

Editing and proofreading are often lumped together, however, there is some distinction between the two. To put it simply, proof-reading deals with more of the technical aspects of the document, such as grammar and spelling, while editing deals more with how well the content itself works (*Editing vs. Proofreading*, n.d.)

So, let's polish that paper. The first thing you want to do is put the paper down. Flip it over, turn the laptop off, and chuck your pencil across the room, but whatever you do, do not engage with your paper before you've had the opportunity to take a break. If you're dealing with a deadline, the very idea of putting it away will probably give you anxiety. However, there is a reason why you need to take a break before you dive back in. You've already been staring at that paper for hours. You need a break to engage with it with fresh eyes. If you dive right into the editing phase, there's a good chance you're going to miss a very noticeable mistake.

Alright, you've taken your break and had a chance to walk away from the paper. Now, you can use your more objective eyes to really get to the brunt of the work. Let's begin with proofreading. To start, consider reading the paper backward as you search for errors. While it may seem odd, this can help you focus on each individual word to check for any spelling errors. Speaking of errors, you should also be prepared for the limits of any digital grammar or spelling checkers. While many of them can give you a good start, they can be a little limited and not always catch mistakes (*Seven Effective Ways to Proofread Writing*, n.d.)

It is also important to consider what time of day you are proofreading. Let's say you leave proofreading until the middle of the night when you're dead tired. If you proofread at a time of day when you are not alert, you are more likely to miss even the tiniest of mistakes (*Tips for Effective Proofreading*, 2009).

Next, we will move on to the editing stage. Remember, by this point, you should be done with the technical aspects of grammar and spelling. At this stage, you need to be checking the sentences for flow, conciseness, redundancy, and clarity. One thing that might help you check all this is reading the paper out loud.

NONVERBAL COMMUNICATION AND BODY LANGUAGE

Do you sometimes notice that when someone is talking to you, something about their mood shifts suddenly? You ask them if something is wrong, but they say everything is totally fine. However, that nagging feeling that something changed still lingers even if verbally they deny anything happened.

Chances are what you noticed is a change in their body language. Our body language may at times be subtle, but that doesn't mean it doesn't convey our true feelings. The field of kinesics has devoted years to researching the nuances of how we communicate non-verbally.

Many times, body language is subtle, so you really have to pay attention and remember there's a lot of subtlety to interpreting what people mean when they don't outright tell you.

Interpreting Nonverbal Signs

Not everybody is good at figuring out what people are conveying with their body language. It's still important to learn because we surprisingly say a lot with the tiniest movements. In fact, some believe that upwards of 93% of communication is done nonverbally (Spence, 2020). That's a lot of talking without really saying anything. How can you possibly keep track?

To start, let's talk about microexpressions. These are the subtle ways you move your body or change your facial expression when you feel even the slightest emotion. It can be anything from a slight brow furrow to a smirk at the corner of your mouth (Ryder, 2021).

With these behaviors being so subtle and minute, it can be challenging to interpret microexpressions. However, there are little clues that can help you out. Let's try the emotion of disgust. Have you ever opened the fridge and found food so old and expired it probably counted as a biohazard? Did it make your eyes narrow or your lips curl over your teeth? All of those are also microexpressions that are made when someone is feeling disgust (Van Edwards, 2013).

When your friend comes up behind you wearing a Halloween mask and scares the living daylights out of you, your eyes probably widen and your eyebrows shoot right up—clear indicators of being surprised. If your mouth dropped open and your forehead creased a bit, that would be an example of actual fear showing on your face (Van Edwards, 2013).

There are also ways to tell if someone is truly invested in what you are saying just by judging their body language. Someone interested in the conversation is going to maintain eye contact, appear physically open (e.g., their posture is straight), and indicate through gestures that they are listening. Whereas, someone who is uninterested is more prone to appearing "closed off" by engaging in body language opposite to an approachable person (Cuncic, 2021).

As with any form of communication, however, context is the crucial part of interpreting someone else's meaning. Consider how the verbal portion of a conversation is playing out before you assume that your conversation partner is upset with you.

For instance, if you said a joke, consider if your friend is suddenly drawing away from you because they found it offensive. There are even other factors that might be at play. Maybe they were listening, but their body language seemed closed off only because they didn't get enough sleep the night before. When in doubt, it never hurts to politely ask someone if you are unsure of their physical reaction.

Apart from body language, there are also other nonverbal cues that can tell you a lot without actually saying anything. Let's look at haptics for a moment. So much can be conveyed through physical touch. For instance, let's say when you were younger, you and your best friend had a secret handshake. It was something just for the two of you to convey how close your bond was. Doing the exact same handshake with other people—even if they are also close to you—wouldn't feel the same way.

Another way to communicate silently is through proxemics. Think of it like the concept of personal space. When we don't really know someone that well, our bubble around them can be an indicator of how close to them we feel. When someone makes us uncomfortable, we might even move farther away from them. Whereas, with our close friends or family, we generally don't mind being physically closer. This is, of course, very dependent on personal preference. There are also other factors with how haptics convey messages, such as cultural and social norms (Cherry, 2023).

Even objects and things can be a form of communication about what a person values the most. For instance, let's say that being a soccer player is a huge part of your identity. How do you convey that? Well, the poster of your favorite player in your room is one physical object that might give it away. Even digital things such as profile pictures or avatars can convey a lot about your identity and personality without you actually saying anything at all (Cherry, 2023). This can be a great tool when you're first meeting someone.

Let's say that you have to do a class exercise with another student you haven't interacted with very much easy-to-recognize before. You need to find an icebreaker quickly if you want to avoid any awkwardness. That's when you notice that they are wearing a pin from an easy-to-recognize TV show. You may not even watch it yourself, but it gives you something to lead the conversation with. Maybe, you'll even get a new show recommendation out of it!

There are also paralinguistics. This one can be a little confusing because it's kind of verbal and also kind of not. You know when go, "Hmm?" when you didn't quite catch something someone else said? That is an example of paralinguistics. They aren't words per se but, rather, sounds that convey meaning (Cherry, 2023).

The scope of nonverbal communication we do daily is quite extensive. Stop and take a moment to look for some of these little cues. You may be surprised at how much you'll come to understand about other people when you start to pay attention to the subtle cues here and there.

REFLECTION

When you want something, you have to convey what you want to other people. When you're trying to solve a problem, you need to be able to talk to each other without it turning into a destructive blowout. Communication is central to the dynamics between you and other human beings.

Now, it's time to put these conversation skills to the test. Next time you have a conversation with someone, pay attention to some of the things discussed. Something else you can try is to repeat back what you understood your conversation partner to have said. For example, "What I heard you say was..." This will not only make sure you are engaging your active listening skills but will also nip any miscommunication in the bud. If you did miss something, this gives the other person the perfect opportunity to clarify their point.

Also, be sure to pay attention to your conversation partner's body language. For example, do they lean forward or away from you when you're talking? When you notice things like that, you can determine how invested they are in what you are saying. If they are showing disinterest, you can try to get their attention back or change the conversation to a different topic altogether.

4

DIGITAL LITERACY AND ONLINE SAFETY

The internet is a complicated thing. In theory, it is a highway of information and connection. However, it has its dark side. A startling 36% of people claim that they have experienced some form of cyberbullying. When it comes to teenagers, that number jumps to a whopping 60%, with 87% having at least seen some form of cyberbullying (*51 Critical Cyber Bullying Statistics in 2019*, 2022).

Cyberbullying isn't the only issue the internet has to contend with. Some form of attack on the internet that compromises safety or privacy occurs roughly every 39 seconds. In 2020, millions of Americans also had their identities stolen through the theft of their private information. And most harrowing of all is the fact that one in seven minors comes into contact online with someone intending to sexually abuse them (Muntingh, 2021).

Alright, we know you've probably heard this lecture more than once. "The internet is a scary and dangerous place. You never know who you can trust, because everyone lies on the internet. "We also know that the internet on its own isn't a bad thing. However, the problem is that the internet is populated by people—and people are an entirely different matter.

For example, there is the issue of internet scams. Seemingly harmless links and pop-ups can very easily turn into phishing scams. As soon as all your information is lost, it becomes a headache to deal with, especially if it goes to the extent of identity theft.

In the modern digital world, good digital literacy can save you a lot of headaches and protect you from a variety of dangers.

INTERNET SAFETY AND PRIVACY

The internet is home to much of humanity's greatest expression of thought, art, science, and debate. It is also home to places that can get you in trouble. Without sugar-coating it, there are a lot of websites that can put your life in danger or put you at risk of getting into serious legal trouble.

Viruses, scams, and the matter of privacy are big issues on the internet. While there's no reason to be scared of the internet itself, knowing what to look out for and how to keep yourself safe can not only save you from minor inconveniences, but it may also save your life. Literally.

Protect Your Information and Privacy

Sometimes, we forget that other people can see what we are doing on the internet. That's why it is critical to guard your personal information at all costs. To start, avoid sharing anything private and personal, especially any information that can be used to find out where you live or give access to your bank accounts (Communications Security Establishment, 2020). This includes any telling pictures as well. You would be amazed at how much information can be found just from an innocent post about, for example, what schools you have or are currently attending.

Oversharing even seemingly harmless things can cause a lot of problems. Say you're going on vacation, so you mention that you're going to Mexico for two weeks. Sounds pretty tame, right? Except when a dedicated hacker can figure out your address, you've just announced that your house and all its belongings are the perfect target for a robbery (Communications Security Establishment, 2020).

As we'll discuss later on, people have ways of finding that information through viruses or hacking. How can you prevent your information from being leaked even unintentionally? Your best friend when it comes to keeping your information a secret is in the passwords you use for all your online accounts (*How to Avoid Sharing Too Much Information Online*, 2021).

You know how when you're making an account for something and you have to make a password that's so many characters long, and it has to have at least one number and one symbol behind it? Well, that's because it's prompting you to make a strong password well-known. Strong passwords are usually hard to guess. In other words, maybe don't use something like a well-known meme or your birthday as a password. Password length is also crucial for protecting your accounts. Shorter passwords tend to be a lot easier to figure out, as opposed to longer passwords. It's also important to make sure that you use different passwords for different accounts or anything you use online (Bender, n.d.). If you use one password for everything, you may as well hand a hacker your information on a silver platter, especially if you make it really easy to guess.

Beyond passwords, the next thing you want to do to keep your accounts safe is to set up two-step authentication. Basically, this is like when you change your email password and get a text message on your phone to verify that you, indeed, are the one requesting the change, as opposed to some stranger (Bender, n.d.).

Identify Scams

Have you heard the one about your long-lost relative, the Nigerian Prince who needs a bit of money to get back on his feet? It's one of the most infamous examples of scams on the internet. Some people will use any tools at their disposal to take advantage of the uninformed. Unfortunately, the internet is no exception to this rule.

There are many different types of scams on the internet, each with its own means of attacking users. Let's take a look at the most common type of scam: malware. Malware is basically the technical term for a computer virus designed to steal information or otherwise disrupt the use and function of another person's computer or internet (Stouffer, 2021). Much like the viruses that humans can contract, there are many different strains of malware.

The next form of malware is Trojan. Trojans are a little different from other forms of malware in the sense that they need you to gain access. Seems rather sneaky, doesn't it? So how do you recognize a Trojan? Always be wary of any suspicious pop-ups you get on your computer. Often, a Trojan can appear as a pop-up claiming that your computer has a virus and you immediately need to take action to fix the issue. What actually happens instead is that you're downloading the problem right onto your computer (Stouffer, 2021).

Another form of malware is spyware. This particular type of malware does exactly what its namesake implies. By hacking into your computer, the virus can use any information on there to monitor you and your online activities. In a similarly threatening vein, there is also ransomware, which exists to trick you into giving up personal information or money under some form of fake duress (Stouffer, 2021).

Finally, there is adware. You know when you get those annoying little pop-ups advertising something and they don't seem to go away no matter how many times you click them? That's exactly what adware is (Stouffer, 2021).

Imagine for a moment that you get an email claiming you won't be able to use your credit card until you pay a certain "fine." Now, you don't remember incurring any fine to begin with, but the email is very clear that there will be serious consequences if you don't comply, including losing your credit card altogether.

That is exactly the kind of motive a ransomware virus would employ.

Aside from malware, there are also phishing scams. A phishing scam is when someone is trying to get you to give up any personal information that they can use against you. Many viruses in some way are phishing scams, but not all phishing scams are viruses. Often, the perpetrator tries to trick the victim with legitimate-looking texts or emails. For example, one tactic might be a message saying that there has been "suspicious login activity" for an account. They will then try to get you to give up this information voluntarily in order to correct the issue. Another example is claiming that you need to correct some financial information (*How to Recognize and Avoid Phishing Scams*, 2019).

A good rule of thumb to avoid being phished is to simply ask yourself if you know the "company" or have an account with them. If the answer is a hard "no," do not engage with the email or text further. If it looks legitimate, however, a good rule of thumb is to contact the company directly to confirm the matter through an official representative (*How to Recognize and Avoid Phishing Scams*, 2019).

All of this sounds scary. However, if you use common sense and trust your gut, you can easily avoid falling prey to any of these scams. Remember, if something seems suspicious, there is a good reason you're getting that vibe. If you believe that you might have fallen victim to any type of scam, it's important to contact the Federal Trade Commission for assistance (Deutsch, 2019).

Surf Safely

Now, we don't want you to throw away your computer and set the remains on fire. There are many reasons to use the internet and many positives from it. You can still enjoy surfing the web, and there are lots of things you can do to keep yourself and your information safe while browsing.

The first step is to make sure that your computer is secure. To do this, you can easily download antivirus software (Communications Security Establishment, 2020). How do you know which software is right for you?

There are a few key things to look for. To start with, many antivirus software programs have some sort of payment plan. It is important to note that you can often find "free" antivirus software. While that may be tempting when on a budget, it's important to be wary, as there is a strong chance that it's a front for a virus downloading or phishing scam. It's also important that you make sure the antivirus software scans for multiple types of suspicious content (*How to Evaluate Anti-Virus Software (and Choose the Right One for You)*, 2020).

It's also important to keep in mind who you are talking to on the internet. At the tamest, the person on the other side of the screen is just someone looking for you to send them money while promising to meet you and never following through. However, it can get much more dangerous than someone trying to catfish you for an easy lump sum. Child predators often use the internet to connect with children in their target age groups (*Internet Safety for Kids: Staying Safe from Online Predators*, 2019).

There are many signs you might be talking to a predator online. They might request inappropriate images or videos or even want to know your location. When they don't get their way, they sometimes resort to threatening their victims. They may also message you things that make you feel uncomfortable or unsafe (*Internet Safety for Kids*, 2019).

DIGITAL FOOTPRINT AND REPUTATION MANAGEMENT

Have you ever heard the phrase, "What happens on the internet, stays on the internet"? The scope of that phrase makes it hard to comprehend, but let's look at an example. Imagine that your friend posts a video of them shoplifting from a convenience store. To be rather blunt, there's no stupider thing she could have done. What would happen when she applies for a summer job and her potential employer happens to see that video? What about her parents? Or the police for that matter.

What if she took the video down? Unfortunately, even that wouldn't be enough to undo what's already occurred. There are many ways for other people to save for posts and videos, and the original poster has absolutely no control over them.

Of course, this can also cause a lot of danger for people when it comes to the leaking of personal information. Countless people take advantage of the naivete of others sharing things online in order to hurt them.

However, we're going to give you the education and tools so you can ensure that nothing like this ever happens to you.

What Is a Digital Footprint?

When people say "the internet is forever," they aren't saying that for no reason. Everything you do on the internet does, in fact, remain traceable. This is a concept known as the digital footprint. Every post, everything you share or like, and the data you use—all of it can be classified as your digital footprint.

There are two different types of digital footprints: active and passive. Active digital footprints are what you put on the internet intentionally. This includes anything you put on social media, the data you allow to be shared and stored, and any information you voluntarily give to sign up for accounts and services. A passive digital footprint is all the hidden bits of data and information that can be traced back to your IP address (*Digital Footprint*, 2022).

We really can't stress enough that when we mean this stuff can be linked back to you, there can be some serious consequences. What you put on the internet can either be a boon or a bane to your reputation. A negative digital footprint can cost you anything from losing out on jobs and scholarships to outright legal consequences.

Good Digital Image and Reputation

If you turned a little pale at the idea of everyone judging you based on what you put on the internet, you're taking the consequences of your digital footprint seriously. The good news is that you can still enjoy the internet and avoid the negative pitfalls. The key to not having your social media and accounts come back to haunt you is to have a good digital image and reputation.

There are many simple ways for you to put out a good digital image/reputation. Primarily, it's all about how you present yourself in what you post. We're not saying that you have to dress up in business clothes and have zero facial expressions. Being silly and having fun is part of life. However, be mindful that how you present yourself affects how people perceive you. What that can mean is to avoid sharing any images of you engaging in dangerous or illegal activities, in compromising positions, or wearing age-inappropriate attire (Eaton, 2011).

Speaking of dangerous activities, let's talk about the elephant in the digital room. These days, it always appears as if there is some new, often dangerous or highly stupid, challenge that goes viral. Why do so many teenagers engage in such hazardous activities? When we are young, we're still trying to figure out the tricks of socializing with our peers. So often, teenagers will do something unsafe to appear as if they belong with their peers who are doing the same thing. Even if by some miracle you don't get severely hurt following a dangerous internet challenge, you definitely gain a reputation for being an idiot.

Another thing to maintain your reputation is to consider who might see the things you post online. If you wouldn't show the picture or video to your parents or future boss, strongly reconsider whether or not it should be online in the first place (Ben-Joseph, 2018). This includes anything we already mentioned and could also include the language you use or the comments you make online.

Responsible Social Media Use and Digital Citizenship

Social media is a complicated thing. There are many positives about it, but the key to keeping your social media experience positive is by using it responsibly. When you know how to engage with social media in a safe manner, you can generate a positive digital space for yourself and others. That way, you can enjoy all those positives while minimizing your chances of engaging with the negative aspects of social media.

The first step is to look at your accounts. Are they private? If not, you should consider making them private (Grossel, 2020). Yes, the internet was made for sharing things with a lot of people. However, there are benefits to keeping your accounts private. Think of it like limiting the amount of people likely to see certain things you post. Consider when you're applying for jobs. Do you really want your future potential boss to look at an account that you mostly share with friends? Probably not. Making that account private, however, will reduce the chances of anyone you don't want seeing what you get up to online.

Then there's being mindful of what you're posting. Always stop and consider the question: "Should I be posting/sharing this?" Really let that question sink in. Consider what that post or share is going to lead to. Are people going to think differently of you if you post it? Could it in any way negatively affect your reputation or safety?

It's also important to be mindful of how much social media you are consuming. Too much of anything can be detrimental to your health. In fact, some studies suggest that teenagers who engage with social media more than three times a day are more likely to experience mental health issues (Mayo Clinic Staff, 2022).

But the internet is so much more than just social media. The internet, for all its good and bad, is a community. It's a very big community, mind you, and there's no way to make it 100% perfect. There's not even a foolproof way to make sure it's safe. When you think of it like a community, you quickly realize that you aren't simply an internet user, you're also a digital citizen. You can do your part to make being online more enjoyable, not only for you but for other users as well.

Good digital citizenship use starts by being mindful of what you put out on the internet. In the same vein, it's also important to not overshare. It's just not smart to do something like put your entire address and location on social media (Grossel, 2020). Beyond human trafficking issues, you are making it very easy for people who mean any kind of harm to find you.

Oversharing doesn't have to be only about critical information like that. If you're feeling really emotional, for example, it may be time to put the social media away until you are feeling calmer (Grossel, 2020). There are many reasons for this. First as harsh as it may sound, it can be a bit of a headache for other people when we are constantly talking about only the negative parts of our lives on social media. While your friends and loved ones will obviously care about you if you are struggling, it's also a lot for people to deal with when you publicly broadcast all your problems for the world to see.

Not only that but there is a very strong chance that if you're posting while feeling emotional, you may wind up saying something you will later regret. When passions run high, we can sometimes forget that little filter in the back of our brains telling us that we should dial it back a bit.

It is also important to do your part to create a safe and positive space for other internet users. What does this mean? To start, do not under any circumstances engage in or cyberbullying others. This means do not engage in any behavior that encourages abuse or the spread of threatening messages. It can also involve spreading slander or rumors about others. Many negative effects can result from cyberbullying, for both the victim and the perpetrator. In certain countries or areas, the laws against cyberbullying are so severe that anyone engaging in it can face legal consequences (*Cyberbullying: What Is It and How to Stop It*, n.d.). If in doubt, always remember the golden rule: If you wouldn't like anybody treating you in a certain way, do not treat others in that manner.

Another thing you can do to be a good digital citizen is to report any negativity you encounter in digital spaces that could greatly affect yourself or other users. For instance, if you see illegal or unsafe activity or encounter any form of cyberbullying, you should report it to the appropriate authorities (Grossel, 2020).

CRITICAL EVALUATION OF ONLINE INFORMATION

Have you ever heard of a town crier? Basically, a town crier was a person who would go around shouting about relevant news and announcements to their community (Castelow, 2017).

Now, our analogy may be a little archaic, but hear us out on this one. Think of the internet as having millions of town criers all shouting different things at the same time. With all that noise, how do you figure out which voice you can trust and should pay attention to?

When anyone can have a platform on the internet, that also means that people can say virtually anything they want—even if that information isn't accurate or truthful in the slightest. In one survey taken in 2022, around 42% of people expressed concerns about the accuracy of the news they were seeing on social media (Watson, 2023). The scary thing is, if you look at some of the numbers, they aren't unjustified in their concerns. Another survey showed that 44% of journalists have discovered news that they were led to believe was in some way fabricated (Watson, 2022).

The thing is, these people putting out all this fake information online can be very persuasive. If they weren't, no one would fall for any false information or news put on the internet. Fortunately, with some skills and a little bit of critical thinking, you can sort out which information is the truth.

Discerning Reliable Information

It's an understatement that there's a ton of information on the internet. Trying to figure out who's accurate and who's spouting nonsense, well, it can really make your head spin. Fortunately, there are many ways to filter information.

The first step is to determine where the information is coming from. For the peak of accuracy, you should consider whether the source of the information is coming from a well-researched scholarly source. There are a lot of ways you can determine whether or not the information you are viewing is academically researched. One particularly big green flag for a researched/scholarly source is that it will have some form of a references page (*How to Identify Reliable Information Online*, 2023). If it doesn't have any references, it makes it that much harder for the information to be fact-checked.

Remember when we mentioned that in all essays you needed to back up your argument with facts? The same rules apply to anything that claims to be "fact." If they can't back it up with some kind of link or reference to a study, chances are it may be questionable in its reliability.

There is also the issue of whether or not the source has been peer-reviewed (*How to Identify Reliable Information Online*, 2023). In academic fields, experts are always reviewing the works of others to determine if they are accurate and well-written. If something you have been searching for isn't peer-reviewed, that means no one else has looked into it. Think of it like someone giving an extra stamp of approval on its accuracy.

But, of course, you aren't going to be on the internet just to find academic sources. There are other things that you need to fact-check, including news articles. After all, there are millions of different news websites. How can you tell which one is actually telling the truth as opposed to just copy-pasting some conspiracy theory Twitter thread?

You also have to remember that even with the best of intentions, there is a lot of bias on the internet. Consider a rumor spreading around your school. If you like the person being gossiped about, are you as likely to believe the rumor as you would be if you hated their guts? The same applies to the internet. Personal bias can often get in the way of information being spread (Kaspersky, 2021). Once it gets going, it becomes difficult to contain. Take conspiracy theories, for example. If you disagree with someone spouting absolute nonsense, they're more likely to double down, insisting that your denial is just proof there's some greater truth being covered up.

So, how can you tell if the information you're looking at is biased? You have to employ a little bit of critical thinking to get there. Let's say you are reading an article about whether or not the minimum wage should be raised. Consider for a moment, who is writing the article? Is it from a company that might benefit from not giving their employees higher wages? Are both sides of the argument presented? Do they list the pros and cons of either raising or maintaining the minimum wage? Does the article seem as though it's leaning extremely one way and presenting opinion rather than facts? All of those can be signs that you are looking at biased information (*Research Guides: How to Evaluate Information*, 2019).

Another thing you can do to arm yourself against misinformation is to educate yourself as much as possible. When you go to a doctor, do you think they got their medical license by reading one textbook? Of course not! They go through numerous classes and a variety of learning tools and materials to gain that information. The same rule applies to the internet. For example, say you are trying to read up on a type of medication.

There may be many people who have a distrust of doctors on the internet and might spread false information about the medication. However, if you take time to gather information and educate yourself, you can draw your own conclusions.

When someone wants to convince you that something incorrect is a fact, they get very good at lying. That's why it's especially important that you learn to fact-check information (Government of Canada, 2023). Imagine that you're doing a science project on boa constrictors. You do online research but stumble upon a website that incorrectly claims that constrictor snakes kill their prey with venom. A very quick Google search, however, will fact-check that and tell you that constrictor snakes squeeze their prey so tightly that it cuts off blood flow (Bittel, 2015).

There are a variety of methods you can use to fact-check information. First, consider the qualifications of the article author. When you are reading up on an article about mental health, chances are you would prefer someone with credentials in psychology, such as a PhD (Kaspersky, 2021)). If it's written by "Jane Doe," with no credentials, there may likely be incorrect information.

Another thing you can do is check how old the article is (Spencer, 2022). Human knowledge is a constantly evolving thing. It wasn't that long ago when you think about it when arsenic was being given as a health remedy (Paul et al., 2022). If you're looking at information that seems pretty dated, it may be time to look for more up-to-date intel.

Critically Navigating the Internet

Part of existing in the digital age is knowing when and how to navigate the internet. Part of that is learning to recognize when you should not be using a particular website. Some websites are definitely safe and legitimate websites that serve some degree of purpose. However, there are many websites that are made to only look legitimate on the surface level. Those websites have far more sinister purposes behind them.

We've already talked a little bit about how to spot fake information, but now we will take it a step further and talk about how to determine whether a website you are using is legitimate enough. This is very important because illegitimate websites can greatly affect your safety.

The first step to determining whether a website is safe is by examining the URL. If it's a URL you might recognize but it's spelled wrong, for example, it could be a phishing attempt in disguise. Always check if the URL has "https" at the beginning or contains a lock icon. Both of these signify that the website is secure (*How to Identify and Protect*, n.d.).

Another indicator of a legitimate website is whether or not it contains an "About Us" segment (*How to Identify and Protect Yourself*, n.d.). Think about it: Legitimate websites want to tell you as much about themselves as they can. If the website is shady, the last thing they want is you asking too many questions about who they really are or what the website's mission is.

There are other things to look out for with websites as well. Take a close look at the website. Any legitimate blog or business or what have you will spend time and money to make sure their website is well designed. Chances are, someone who's looking to scam you isn't going to put in as much time or effort on that. If the website appears low quality for any reason, you may want to ask yourself why a website with good intentions would have such crummy graphics. Some other key things to look out for are excessive pop-up ads, links to other unknown sites or pages, and typos (*5 Quick Tips for Navigating the Internet Like a Pro*, 2017).

All in all, your best friend when determining the safety of a website is common sense. Chances are if something seems off, or worse someone is trying to offer you something that just seems a little too wonderful, leave the website as quickly as possible.

REFLECTION

Now, you are properly equipped with knowledge about the dangers and risks that exist online. To ensure that you're use of the internet keeps you safe and secure, it's time for you to set yourself some ground rules.

Think of five do's and don'ts regarding rules you can implement to keep yourself safe on the internet. This can be what websites are okay to use or rules about how you use social media (Ben-Joseph, 2018).

Let's say we're talking about putting pictures online. Consider rules for what you should and should not post. When you are taking pictures, it's important to consider what type of images are appropriate for other people to see (Eaton, 2011). If it falls under any of the categories we mentioned of what not to put online, consider it part of a "don't" rule.

5

FINANCIAL LITERACY AND MONEY MANAGEMENT

D o you know how money works? It seems like a relatively simple concept. To get things, you need to have and exchange money. However, it's a lot more complicated than that. In fact, many teenagers don't have a sound grasp of financial literacy at all. Almost 75% of teenagers report that they don't feel confident in their financial literacy when it comes to their personal finances (Turner, 2023). In addition, 25% of students don't learn finances from their families, and in the United States, only 23 states have some form of financial literacy integrated into the school curriculum (Turner, 2023).

The problem doesn't only have something to do with the inexperience of youth. Even adults run into trouble due to a lack of financial literacy. In 2021, many Americans reported losing a significant amount of money because of their lack of financial knowledge (Turner, 2023). When you consider that, it becomes abundantly clear that many people lack fundamental financial knowledge.

We don't guarantee any of these tips are going to make you filthy rich. However, when you have proper knowledge of budgeting, credit, investing, and saving, you will be surprised to see how much your finances benefit in the long term.

BUDGETING AND FINANCIAL PLANNING

More money in your pocket is always preferable—especially when you have your eye on something expensive that you really want, like a new video game or a car, let's say. That's not even getting into all the things teenagers should ideally be saving up for once they finish high school. If you plan to go to college, there's tuition and textbooks to start. Then, if you're living away from home to attend school, there are expenses such as rent/dorm fees, transportation, and groceries. Even if you try to save money, sometimes you just end up still flat-out broke.

The best way to save up money is through good budgeting and financial planning.

Creating a Personal Budget

Whether you have some form of allowance from your parents or receive pay from an after-school job, you know the money in your pocket is yours to do with as you please. However, now that you're starting to spend your own money, you are slowly coming to the realization that it is finite. You have to keep in mind how much you have when you are making any kind of purchase to make sure you aren't completely flushing hundreds of dollars down the drain.

That is why you need to learn how to budget. A budget is basically having an idea of how much money you have to spend within a certain framework in a certain period of time (Ganti, 2023). Let's look at your parents. What would their monthly budget look like? Well, they would need to figure out what expenses they need to cover for the month, and that would be their budget, with maybe some slight room for flexibility in case of an emergency or to leave room for a frivolous/fun purchase.

One way you can simplify the budgeting process is by following the 50-30-20 rule. To put it simply, you spend the largest portion of your budget (50%) on things that can be classified as urgent needs. Then, you spend the next portion (30%) on things you may want but are not classified as essential needs. Finally, the remaining 20% should be spent on reducing any debt you have or may gain in the near future (Smith & Underwood, 2023).

Let's say you have a budget of $100. Following this setup, you would spend $50 on food, $30 on buying new headphones, and $20 to go toward paying off your credit card—or you can save that portion for a rainy-day fund. It is, however, important to note that if you are living in a low-income situation, this particular model might be difficult to follow (Smith & Underwood, 2023). So, let's say that you have $100, but you need $60 to go towards rent. Well, that already skews your whole budget.

When making a budget, you should consider several factors. Start with what your income is. That is how much money you have to work with. Now, consider what you want to do with it —whether that means saving the money, spending it, or paying off any debts. Bills and mandatory expenses should also be put into play (Ganti, 2023).

Now comes the tricky part. You need to come up with a spending plan (Ganti, 2023). Let's say you have $1,000 to work with. You need to pay off a credit card and pay rent, so that's $500, let's say. The remaining $500 is left for you to have free reign to either save or spend on things that are not immediate or important.

Financial Goals and Budgeting

Budgeting is one of the key factors that can help you achieve your financial goals. The point of budgeting is to track your expenses over a period of time. This makes it ideal for keeping track of whether you are following your financial goals (Fontinelle, 2021).

You are also going to have to allow for some flexibility when it comes to budgeting. If you make a monthly budget, no month is going to turn out the same. Plus, you have to account for any potential emergency spending that can easily pop up. For example, if something happens to your car and you have to pay to get it fixed. However, by looking at your budget after dealing with that, you can best figure out where you need to redirect your money to get back on track (Fontinelle, 2021).

One way you can prepare for any potential pitfalls of unexpected expenditures is by creating an emergency fund. This way, when the unexpected happens, you know that you have coverage. It also makes getting back on track to achieving your financial goals that much easier (Fontinelle, 2021).

If you haven't already, the first step to understanding financial goals and budgeting is to create your own bank account (Ganti, 2023). When you set up your very first bank account, you'll need to have various forms of identification readily available. These include proof of residency/address, government-issued I.D. (such as a passport or driver's license), and your social security number (*Opening a Bank Account*, 2017). Then, it's simply a matter of going to the bank and filling out the right forms.

Saving Strategies and Smart Spending Habits

The first thing you should do if you want to start saving money is open a savings account (Knueven, 2022), but not just any savings account. A regular savings account can be a good way to save money, but you don't just want "good" savings. You want the best savings you can get. That's why the best way you can accumulate your money is through a high-yield savings account. These are savings accounts that have a higher interest rate than your average savings account (Adams, 2022). In other words, when you put money into one of these, your account grows faster than it would with a basic savings account.

The opposite end of the spectrum to saving is *spending* money. While the ideal way to save is to not spend any money at all, we realistically know that's wishful thinking. However, if you're smart about how you spend your money, it's a whole different story.

Find ways to gradually start cutting back on expenses. Eventually, you are going to also be responsible for your own household expenses. Living on your own and footing all of the bills/rent really starts to add up. When it comes to household expenses, it's important to know how to save a few dollars. For example, when shopping for groceries, you can save money by using coupons. You can even use this for fun spending by shopping for things that are on sale (Knueven, 2022).

It isn't even just common sense but an actual fact that avoiding impulsive spending can benefit your bank account. Several studies have shown that when methods were taken to employ self-control on spending, it had a tremendous effect on finances (Davydenko et al., 2021). This can look different for everyone, but it might involve things like making sure you carry cash with you when you want to spend money. This helps make sure you're more mindful of how much you have to spend. It might also mean severely cutting back on buying things you might consider a "need" as opposed to a "want."

UNDERSTANDING CREDIT AND DEBT

Even a lot of adults can have a hard time understanding how the world of finance and banking works. The terminology certainly doesn't help. Fortunately, at this point, you don't need to worry about intensely complicated terms like "escrow." However, what you should have a decent grasp on is the concept of credit and debt.

Basics of Credit

Credit can be very easy to understand. The best way to think of it is by looking at what a credit card is. When you pay with a credit card, you are essentially saying, "I have this money but not right now, and I will eventually have to pay it off later on my credit card bill." So, in a sense, credit is borrowing money you don't "yet" have with the expectation that you will repay that later on (The Investopedia Team, 2020).

There are also many different types of credit. One of the most common forms of credit is a loan. A loan is basically an agreement between a borrower and a lender that the borrowed money will be repaid charges. More often than not, loans also come with interest charges (Kagan, 2019b). In other words, the longer you go without paying your debt, the more your debt grows over a period of time.

To get a loan, you have to go through certain processes. To begin with, you need to apply at a bank or some other lending corporation (i.e., a student loan foundation) (Kagan, 2019b). Then, you will have to provide as much of your financial information as possible, including the reason you are taking out a loan in the first place. After that, it's all left up to the bank or corporation to decide if they are going to give you the loan.

When you're applying for a loan, the lender may need you to meet certain requirements before they give you the money. For example, you may be required to have a certain income. They will likely check if you have a good credit history to give them an indication that you'll be able to pay the loan back. Depending on the circumstances of the loan, they may also set up something as collateral to encourage you to pay back the loan at the risk of losing something else (Kagan, 2019b).

Whether or not a loan requires collateral often depends on what the loan is being used for. Let's say you take out a loan to buy a car. The collateral in this case is essentially whether or not you're getting a car at the end of paying off the loan (Kagan, 2019b).

Chances are if you have a basic knowledge of loans, you may be familiar with the concept of loan sharks. It's really important that you know how to recognize them to avoid getting yourself into a sticky situation involving money. A loan shark is a type of lender that often preys on borrowers with ridiculously high interest rates and may resort to unsavory means of ensuring that you pay them back (Kagan, 2019a).

Beyond the employment of high interest rates, loan sharks can also be recognized by the fact that they often do not have the same interest in checking your credit and financial background (Kagan, 2019a). If anyone is offering to lend you money without these checks in place, consider that a blinking neon sign urging you to run the other way.

Responsible Borrowing and Managing Debt

Nearly everyone has to borrow money at some point in their lives. However, when you start to really get into financial literacy it's a lot more complicated than giving five dollars to your friend and telling them they can pay you back "whenever." To understand borrowing, you first need to understand how debt works. When you borrow money, the money you owe back is referred to as debt. There are many different types of debt—one of the most common being credit card debt—but it can also include any kind of loan (Chen, 2003).

While debt definitely does not sound ideal, there are instances in which debt can be beneficial. For many, they might not be able to get many things in life if they did not take them out on a loan. Sometimes, emergencies pop up that require a large amount of money to handle (Chen, 2003). Say, for example, your water heater broke. Your credit card might just be the thing that saves you from having to take cold showers.

However, in that kind of situation, you still need to weigh the pros and cons. Ask yourself if you can really afford to go into debt to get the thing you want to purchase. The unfortunate thing about debt is that if you aren't careful, it can very quickly add up and present serious risks, including but not limited to bankruptcy (Chen 2003). That's why it's important to know how to manage debt and ideally overcome it.

The first rule to prevent debt is to avoid it happening to you in the first place. Consider whether or not you really need to use your credit card for that purchase or if you should take out a loan. If you think you would be better off paying for something by saving up until you have the money for it, that's the recommended option.

Sometimes, debt is completely unavoidable. So, say you've gotten yourself into a bit of debt. Here's what you need to do: Take a look at your income and devote a good chunk of it to paying off the debt (Chen, 2003). Remember, in many cases, debt comes with interest attached. The sooner you can devote your funds to clearing your debt, the better. That way, you can avoid getting into a loop where you can't get ahead of your interest rates.

When you make debt payments also matters. This overlaps with maintaining a good credit score, but you can avoid increasing interest on your credit if you make sure you pay at least the minimum, if not more than the minimum, on time (Chen, 2003).

You can also consider your debit-to-credit limit ratio. In other words, be responsible with exactly how much you borrow compared to your existing credit limit. Let's say you have a limit of $100 for credit. An ideal ratio for many lenders would be that you borrow no more than $30 (Chen, 2003).

Build a Good Credit History and Avoid Financial Pitfalls

Why is a good credit history so important? Being able to maintain a good credit score is a litmus test for how well you're able to manage debt. When you prove that you can responsibly manage debt, you also show that you can handle receiving a loan. In other words, if for whatever reason you need to petition for a loan, you're more likely to succeed if your credit score is good (Lake, 2022).

To maintain a good credit history, it's sometimes best to leave it in the hands of professionals. There are many services that exist to monitor your credit scores. Do you find that you're still having a lot of trouble with your credit? Consider speaking to a credit counselor in person to advise you on the next steps to take.

The good news is that you don't necessarily need to make the full payment for your credit card bill. As long as you are making your monthly payments on time, you are still able to showcase responsible debt management. Even paying only the minimum payment has no repercussions on your credit history; however, paying the amount in full will improve your credit score even more (Lake, 2022).

The first rule to keep in mind is to never borrow more money than you can pay off. Try not to spend more than what your credit limit is worth (*Improving Your Credit Score*, 2016). Let's say you have $500 in cash. Would you try to buy something worth $10,000? No, because that would be completely shortsighted. Mind how you spend money with your credit card to avoid potentially hurting your score with something you can't pay off.

INVESTING AND BUILDING WEALTH

Full transparency: Everyone prefers more money as opposed to less money. That's why investing can be an important step in building your wealth over time. The concept of investing can seem intimidating, but it is actually quite simple. Investing is basically when you put your money toward something in the hopes that sometime in the future even more money will be returned to you (Picardo, 2022).

Many teenagers struggle with the concept of investing. Often, the issue stems from the fact that investing is time-consuming and can be confusing to break down (Adams, 2023). At this point, you don't need to get into more complicated types of investments—such as a 401(k), bonds, or escrow—but getting a basic idea of how to invest and gradually build your wealth can save you a lot of money and trouble later on in life.

Investing and Long-Term Wealth Accumulation

There are many different ways to take the wealth you have and make it grow over a period of time. One of the most common ways of doing this is through investing. Investing is putting your money toward something that will make you even more money later on (Picardo, 2022). There are many different types of investments, but we'll explore your options in a bit. First, let's talk about the benefits of investing.

It's pretty self-explanatory that investing can help you build wealth, but there are a few other benefits to it as well. When you start paying taxes, investing can help you save money on tax returns. While that may seem like a long way away and a "future you problem," every penny saved counts.

Long-term financial goals also benefit from investment. Since the idea of investing is to gradually increase your money, it makes sense to use investment to achieve your more long-term financial goals.

Investing, however, is not your only option to make money. You can accumulate your wealth by earning money. This can mean working a job, but it doesn't always have to be something like that. Another way you can accumulate wealth is by considering what you have to offer as an individual (Knueven, 2022). Everyone has something they are really good at. The trick to making good money at it is to market your skills smartly. Now, you may not necessarily be looking to become the next "brilliant young entrepreneur," but there are other ways of accumulating wealth on the side other than starting a business.

Are you really good at a particular subject in school? Why not consider offering your skills as a tutor for a reasonable price? Do you like interacting with kids? Consider babysitting. If you have the time in your schedule to seek part-time work, go for it! The best way to accumulate wealth is by having some or multiple streams of income at your disposal.

Different Investment Options

You really don't need that much convincing that it's a good idea to start saving your money. After all, who doesn't want to make sure they have a few extra dollars on hand for the future? But the real question is, how can you save money when you're still so young? We already know that investing is a good way to accumulate wealth. Fortunately, there are really simple ways you can invest, even when you're young.

To start, let's look at one of the most well-known forms of investment: stocks. A lot of people are under the impression that teenagers can't invest in stocks (Adams, 2022). That's only for the guys in business suits working on Wall Street, right? Well, the good news is you don't have to wait to be an adult to invest in stocks. Granted, you can't do it on your own either. Technically, you *do* have to be an adult to invest in stock under your name. That's why it's a good idea to get your parents on board to act similarly to a broker. They help you accumulate the stock and make stock-related decisions until you reach adulthood and the money becomes yours (Liberto, 2023).

While retirement seems like a long way off, it doesn't hurt to invest in it as soon as possible. When it comes to saving up for that part of your future, you want to invest in a Roth IRA. The trick to a Roth IRA is that you already need to have some kind of income (Tretina, 2023). In other words, if you already have a job, you already have a great head start. The money from your job gets put toward the Roth IRA after taxes have been deducted (Coombes, 2021).

However, the downside to a Roth IRA is that only people within a certain income bracket can apply for one. In other words, there is a cap on how much money you can make in order to apply for it. They can also have restrictions on when and why you can withdraw money without fines or tax deductions, so it's best to keep that in mind if you think you need to dip into it for emergencies (Coombes, 2021).

Future Financial Goals

The future always seems so far away—until all of a sudden, it isn't. That's why planning for future financial goals is so important, even when you are young.

You can make many different financial goals at this point in your life. Depending on how old you are, now is the time to start thinking about expenses such as college. It's an unfortunate truth that for many, student loans are a necessary evil to pay for higher education (Fontinelle, 2021). However, if you start saving with that in mind, you could either reduce the amount you might need or avoid taking out a loan altogether.

Consider other aspects of the future, too. For example, do you want to live in an apartment for your whole life or do you want to own a house someday? Do you plan on financing a wedding in the future? What about having kids? These and other factors are important to consider when planning out future financial goals. Even retirement is something to prepare for (Fontinelle, 2021).

Maybe you're a bit of an entrepreneur. Has it ever been your dream to have your own business? Well, the good news is that you're never too young to start building one! Many well-known people began growing their businesses from a young age. In fact, Facebook creator Mark Zuckerberg was only 19 when he founded one of the most well-known social media platforms (Clifford, 2017).

There are a lot of benefits you can gain from starting a business while young. For one thing, if it does work out, you have an opportunity to really get ahead of the curve and forge your career. In the event it doesn't work out, you still have a lot of time ahead of you to change directions.

Don't be scared of the concept of failure. It can take many failures before a business can get off the ground. However, because you are so young, you have more than enough time to gain the education and experience you will need to succeed.

REFLECTION

Very soon in the future, you'll need to start thinking about what your money is going toward. When you are completely on your own, one of the things you'll have to worry about is how to buy yourself food within a certain budget. Consider trying this as an exercise: Think of all the ingredients you would need to cook a new recipe. After taking note of the ingredients, consider how much each of the items is going to cost (*10 Tips for Planning Meals on a Budget*, n.d.).

Ask yourself, would it have been cheaper to have this meal prepared at home as opposed to going out? When it comes to budgeting for a meal, the answer can vary depending on what is being prepared or the price of the meal at different restaurants (Williams, 2023). It may also depend on whether or not you have some ingredients on hand, as opposed to no ingredients for that particular recipe.

Bonus tip: Examine different stores and their prices. It can amaze you just how much you'll save by looking out for a deal (*10 Tips for Planning Meals on a Budget*, n.d.).

6

HEALTHY LIFESTYLE AND WELL-BEING

Were you aware that up to 60% of your physical or mental health is determined by your lifestyle choices (Farhud, 2015)? Did you know that less than 24% of children ages 6–17 do an hour of physical activity in a day (*Physical Activity Facts*, 2020)? Now, it may be hard to fully grasp just how telling those numbers are. Many people take their health for granted. Physical and mental health are vital for so many different aspects of life. This is especially true regarding children and teenagers.

For example, physical activity has been proven to increase academic performance and success (*Physical Activity Facts*, 2020). There is also strong evidence to suggest that mental health greatly influences academic performance as well (Agnafors et al., 2020). It is also unfortunately true that in the older end of the teenage demographic, suicide is recognized as the fourth leading cause of death. Not only that, but a variety of mental illnesses are the leading cause of illness in young adults (*Mental Health of Adolescents*, 2021).

So far, every life skill we've talked about has been important. However, if you don't know how to take care of your physical and mental health, none of these other skills are going to matter. There are so many factors that can greatly influence our health and lifestyles. Even if you are struggling in terms of either physical or mental health, there are many steps you can take towards improvement.

NUTRITION AND HEALTHY EATING HABITS

One study about the eating habits of Canadian teenagers found that 27% of high school students consumed fast food at least twice a week. Similar data from America showed that 75% of teenagers consume fast food at least once a week (Lillico et al, 2014).

There is a strong connection between what we eat and how we feel mentally and physically. There is so much information out there on what's good for you and what's bad for you that it can start to make your head turn. All this talk about macronutrients and micronutrients, well, it's enough to make anyone's head spin. But good nutrition and healthy eating habits don't have to be complicated.

The Importance of Balanced Nutrition and Healthy Food Choices

In at least one health class, you've probably seen a basic diagram of the food pyramid and have some concept of what foods are considered healthy and nutritious. It's not just a ploy to make kids eat more veggies either. There are many reasons why it's important to eat foods that provide adequate nutrients. When you are in your teenage years, your body is kind of taking its natural growth and development and kicking it into high gear. You rapidly grow and go through changes, meaning your body needs the right fuel to keep up with it all. Chances are, you may have already noticed this, as your appetite also increases during this developmental stage (SickKids Staff, 2019).

Even taking out the factor of your age, there are many other reasons why healthy eating is integral to your well-being. You can greatly reduce your risk for many preventable diseases—including diabetes and heart disease—and even give your immune system a boost.

You may also find that the right nutrition has a significant effect on your energy levels and productivity (*Nutrition, 2022*). Think of your body like your phone and a good diet like the charger. You need the right charging cable or your battery simply won't be able to keep up. When you fuel yourself with the foods necessary to provide adequate nutrition, you're using the right cable and giving your "battery" the juice it needs to keep functioning.

Meal Planning

Do your parents/guardians do the cooking in the household? Well, it might be time to consider getting your hands dirty in the kitchen. Meal planning is a great way to encourage healthier eating. There are many reasons behind this. To begin with, meal planning encourages adding some variety to your diet. Sure, you can technically get a lot of healthy nutrients by eating salads every day, but nobody wants to do that. Meal planning, however, encourages the introduction of more healthy things to add to recipes, such as making use of a wide variety of veggies (Blanton, 2022).

Meal planning also discourages impulsive eating (Blanton, 2022). Now, the odd trip to get a snack from the convenience store isn't going to kill you. But with meal planning, you make more informed food choices, opting for foods that are not only good for you but make you feel good as well.

To plan a meal, there are several things you have to consider. You know when you get really hungry and it starts to make you irritable? Nobody likes being hangry. Fortunately, meal planning can also help prevent that (Blanton, 2022). The key is to deliberately choose foods that are going to keep you fuller for longer periods of time. These include certain carbs and proteins or filling fats, like cheese and yogurt.

Planning ahead can also save you a lot of time, especially if you have a very packed schedule. For example, let's look at your lunch. If you meal plan and get everything organized the night before, imagine how much time you'll save getting ready in the morning. It's even more of a bonus if you cook in batches ahead of time or make use of leftovers.

You can also get the rest of your household involved as well. Play an active part in planning various meals together. Maybe you'll learn some old family recipes or have a fun time bonding with your parents, grandparents, or siblings. All that teamwork will really come in handy when you cook food in batches to stretch it over a period of time.

Healthy Relationships With Food

It is an unfortunate reality that even nutrition and healthy eating has its dark side. Many people think that to eat healthy, they have to be super restrictive with their diet. This can cause a lot of issues, such as feelings of anxiety about eating, binging, and intense feelings of guilt (Davidson, 2020).

That sounds like a completely miserable way to live. Food is meant to be enjoyed and savored. No one wants to put that much time and energy into focusing on what they can't eat. Instead, focus on allowing yourself permission to eat (Davidson, 2020).

Consider this: When a cow is munching on a mouthful of grass, is he really taking the time to enjoy it, or is he just eating it to survive? The human relationship with food is so multifaceted and complex that it would be a shame to not allow yourself to participate in the enjoyment (Davidson, 2020).

To participate in this permissive relationship means you have to come to terms with the fact that no foods are forbidden (Davidson, 2020). Yes, even that slice of pizza is all right. Eating healthy is important, but just because you had a little junk food doesn't mean you "failed." All foods in healthy moderation are completely acceptable.

In a way, this permissive eating is also practicing the concept of mindful eating. Mindful eating doesn't have to involve considering the nutritional value of the food you're consuming or following certain rules like you might see in a particular diet. Rather, the intention of mindful eating is to focus on the act of eating itself (Nelson, 2017). Take time to enjoy every bite. Select ingredients and dishes that you love. You can even make dinner a special event. Use the good plates and eat with music and ambient lighting if you want.

PHYSICAL FITNESS AND EXERCISE

Blake and Marley are two best friends. Of the two, the athletically inclined Blake always seems to have more energy, is more focused on her studies, and seems to be less stressed overall. Marley, meanwhile, is more sluggish and struggles to pay attention during the long school day. Not only that, but Marley also seems to have a hard time managing her built-up stress levels.

It's very clear that there's a relationship between the level of physical activity the girls get and their energy levels and ability to function. But can physical fitness really make that much of a difference?

Importance of Regular Exercise

There are many different kinds of exercise. Neither one is better than the other, and their benefits are mostly dependent on what your own fitness goals are.

One common type of exercise is strength training. The point of strength training is to gradually build your muscles and your body's abilities. Usually, strength-training exercises include activities such as lifting weights, squats, certain stretches, etc. Strength training doesn't only make you stronger. It provides many different benefits to your physical and mental health. On the physical side, strength training can reduce your risk for certain illnesses, such as diabetes, and certain types of cancers (Momma et al., 2022).

Aerobic exercise is pretty much just cardio. The idea of aerobic exercises is to get your heart rate elevated and your blood pumping through your veins, benefitting your cardiovascular health. You can also greatly reduce your chances of getting sick during cold and flu season with aerobic exercise. Much like strength training, aerobic exercises can also reduce your stress and increase your sense of mental fortitude (Mayo Clinic Staff, 2018).

Make a Routine

The thing about exercise is you need to do it regularly. To make sure you're getting in the required amount of exercise for your health and personal fitness goals, you need to make a fitness routine and stick to it.

The first thing to consider when creating a routine is how fit you are to begin with. The last thing you want to do before you even start is risk the chance of burning out or potentially hurting yourself. Some good indicators of your fitness level include your weight, flexibility, and ability to do certain exercises such as push-ups (Mayo Clinic Staff, 2019).

Then, you have to consider what you hope to achieve by creating this routine. What goals are you hoping to accomplish by working out (Mayo Clinic Staff, 2019)?

However, you also want to make sure that you aren't doing the exact same exercise every single day of your routine. Not only are you going to bore yourself out of your mind, but you also run the risk of overworking certain parts of your body. For example, when you work out your muscles, you actually create very fine tears. To build strength, you need to keep allowing these small tears to repair. The more you follow this cycle of muscle hypertrophy, the stronger you get (Tavel, 2023). In other words, if you work your muscles every day, you're missing out on the benefit of giving them a rest every now and again.

Adding variety also helps by keeping you interested in working out and providing even more benefits. Cardio doesn't accomplish the same things weight training does, but if you do a mixture of both, you get the best of both exercises. The recommended level of variety you should achieve is 75-150 minutes of aerobic activity (depending on intensity) weekly and strength training at a minimum of twice a week (Mayo Clinic, 2019).

Exercise and Resiliency/Stress

Exercise has been proven to help build resiliency. In this case, resiliency essentially means the ability to manage and cope with very difficult situations. In one study, research found that people were more resilient during COVID-19 when they engaged in regular exercise, as opposed to when they didn't. They also found that resiliency was influenced by the amount of exercise done, finding participants who did more exercise were more resilient than those who did only a little (Lancaster & Callaghan, 2022).

Nearly any physical activity can help you reduce stress. You don't even have to be athletic to receive the benefits. Sometimes, even just getting your body moving a little bit can do wonders for managing your stress.

Let's look at the relationship between exercise and stress and why it should be an integral part of your stress management. Exercise not only benefits your health and sense of well-being, but it also puts vitality into your routine.

Beyond that, there are many ways that exercise physically combats stress. When you exercise, your endorphin levels get a major boost. Endorphins act as your brain's little happy-feel-good chemical. In the case of running, this rush of chemicals can be referred to as a "runner's high." However, it isn't only found in running. This effect also occurs during many aerobic exercises, such as tennis, or even taking a refreshing hike in nature (Mayo Clinic Staff, 2022b).

Exercise also makes stress easier to manage because in some ways the effects of exercise mimic the effects of stress. Your heart races, and your blood quickens in your veins. It's almost equivalent to a fight-or-flight response. In a way, engaging in exercise allows your body to practice how it copes under stress. This leads to many benefits for your cardiovascular, digestive, and immune systems (Mayo Clinic Staff, 2022b).

Remember the "happy chemical," endorphin? Well, that's not the only part of exercise that can boost your mood. Regular exercise not only can reduce anxiety and depression but also gives you an increased sense of self-assurance and relaxation. (Mayo Clinic Staff, 2022b). Plus, it encourages better sleep. Let's face it, when we're stressed out, many of us can't sleep. Fortunately, exercise is a great way to combat this and what lack of sleep does to your mental health.

No exercise is inherently better than the other. However, the key is partaking in an activity that you enjoy (Mayo Clinic Staff 2022b). It can be boxing, yoga, taking a stroll, fencing, lifting weights—literally anything. The world of exercise is your oyster. Any form of movement can elevate your fitness levels and eliminate or greatly reduce stress. The only thing that matters is that you're enjoying yourself and receiving some kind of physical benefit.

MENTAL HEALTH AND STRESS MANAGEMENT

Many people might look at your stress levels and shrug. They assume because of your age that you don't know how bad it can get, that you don't know what it's like to be stressed and struggling with your mental health. In reality, you may have more experience dealing with mental health problems than some adults.

You don't even have to look at individual countries to know that teenagers are dealing with high levels of mental health problems. Worldwide around one in seven children from preteen to teenage years struggle with some variety of mental illness. When you look at the scope of all that, it can be comforting to know that you aren't alone if you experience any form of mental health issue. Many people in your age group are at high risk for developing a mental illness due to a variety of risk factors (World Health Organization, 2021).

With it being so relevant to teenagers, mental health is just as vital to learn about as physical health. There are many consequences to letting your mental health slip through the cracks and, unfortunately, as we've mentioned, teenagers are very susceptible to those pitfalls.

Signs You Need Help and How to Get It

Sometimes, we don't know that we've gotten so far into a problem until it's too deep for us to get ourselves out. The same is true for mental health. It's kind of like getting stuck in a tarpit. You may not think it's that big of a deal at first until you get so stuck you literally can't move forward anymore.

Fortunately, if you know what to look for, many signs can tell you that you're heading toward the danger zone with regard to your mental well-being. It is important to note that there is still some room for variance depending on your personality, coping mechanisms, and even mental health diagnosis. However, here are some general signs that usually raise a red flag.

Let's take a look at Scott's story. Scott is normally a very happy and enthusiastic guy. However, his friends are noticing he just doesn't seem to have the same kind of pep he normally has. He hasn't been playing as many video games with them, he's been moody and irritable, and at lunch, he doesn't seem to have much of an appetite (*Nine Signs of Mental Health Issues*, 2019).

These are just some of the signs that you might be struggling with your mental health at the moment. Other signs can include turning to substance abuse to cope, severe bouts of anxiety, difficulty sleeping, and any significant, long-term changes in mood or behavior (*Nine Signs of Mental Health Issues*, 2019). If you feel as though you are struggling with any of these, some form of intervention may be necessary to help you get better.

There is one thing that must be stressed as a major red flag with regard to seeking help for your mental health. If at any point you are considering harming yourself, it is not up for debate. If you are feeling suicidal, you need immediate intervention.

Being suicidal often comes with alarming warning signs. Suicidal people often feel a lack of interest in anything, as well as experience symptoms of depression and anger. Sometimes, they even voice that they are having suicidal thoughts or ideation. This can look like outright saying they "wish they were dead" or "everyone would be better off without them" (*Warning Signs*, n.d.).

Maybe reading some of these warning signs has made you realize, "Yeah. I need help." What does help look like when you're struggling with mental health? Well, the answer is simple and not at the same time. What help you receive honestly depends on what is going to work best for you as a person to treat the severity of your condition. The best thing you can do is talk to your doctor and consider your options.

An approach that might benefit you is therapy. Many different approaches to therapy can be taken, including cognitive behavioral therapy, eye movement desensitization and reprocessing, and dialectic behavioral therapy to name a few (Smith, 2020). Ultimately, your therapist and your doctor will decide which approach might benefit you the most, and there is no shame in trying a new approach if you find the one you've been given isn't working.

In more extreme cases, help might mean spending time in hospital. There are many images we have of psychiatric care, thanks to stereotypes and media. However, as long as you are in a location that strives for the best in care and compassion, you are in good hands with professionals.

Along with all the other trials of growing up comes responsibility. Simply put, growing up can cause undue stress. Hopefully, you live a happy life. But what about those times when happiness turns to sadness or when, over time, sadness becomes depression? Or when anger turns to rage?

It's alright if it feels like you aren't okay. You have to be empowered to recognize when and how to get help, especially in cases of experiencing suicidal thoughts. If ever you or someone you know have thoughts of suicide, that's not something to be kept secret. You must tell a teacher, counselor, family member, or any trusted adult in your life. You deserve a helping hand when you are down.

Some resources can get you started on seeking help and educating yourself about suicide. These include The Jason Foundation (*"A Friend Asks" App*, n.d.) and the 988 crisis line (*Suicide Prevention Resources*, 2023).

You are not alone. Someone does care about you. You matter. You make a difference.

Nothing will be the same if you're not here to see it.

How to Cope

There isn't just one method that will magically get rid of your stress and anxiety. If there was, it would probably be bottled and sold for millions. However, that doesn't mean there isn't anything that can make you feel at least a little better and help you get by.

The first step may seem too good to be true. Once we tell you, you're probably going to roll your eyes. The first step to coping with your mental health is simply to accept it (Pombo, 2019).

"But that doesn't do anything!" It's very easy to dismiss this, but there is a solid reason behind this. The idea of "radical acceptance" is to simply accept that you are having a hard time coping with your mental health. Think of it like suddenly finding a poisonous snake in your basement. You can try to deny that it's down there, but the snake has still made a nice cozy home near your water heater. Ignoring it isn't going to get it out of the basement or stop it from biting you if you poke it too much. However, if you admit the snake is there, you can do something about it.

Mental health isn't as easy to get rid of as an unwanted reptilian houseguest. In fact, many people suffer from mental illness for most, if not all, of their lives. But, thankfully, there are many ways to cope once you've gotten to the acceptance stage.

Another thing you can try is reframing your negative thoughts (Pombo, 2019). If you keep allowing yourself to sink into negative thought patterns, well, you're going to remain stuck with negative thoughts. Let's imagine you are feeling down about a mistake you made in homework. Instead of saying "I'm stupid," you can instead say, "I'm still learning."

Sometimes, no advice can replace the best option, asking for help. When you seek out a professional to aid you in recovery, they can give you a variety of coping mechanisms. It might take a while to find one that works for you, but the good news is when you get help, you aren't doing it alone. You have someone there with you to guide you through it (Pombo, 2019).

Self-Care Practices and Creating Positive Mental Well-Being

When you aren't in a good headspace, the very thought of taking care of yourself can seem impossible. However, imagine for a moment you were taking care of a young child or a pet. Would you forgo giving them the needs they require for a healthy and happy life? Of course not! So, why do we do that when it comes to ourselves?

It may sound too easy to be true, but take care of yourself and you'll feel a lot better. But some people can get stuck on what they can do to care for themselves.

You don't have to do absolutely every single tip and trick out there to achieve a sense of well-being. It's important to find what form of self-care works for you. One thing you might consider is taking up a hobby to put your focus into something positive and productive (*Self-Care: 5 Ways to Take Good Care of Yourself*, 2021). It can be gardening, tai chi, art, playing the saxophone, or anything you want.

Sometimes, when you are feeling really down and out, it can make you feel lonely. Another self-care activity you can engage in is a social activity (Cooks-Campbell, 2022). Connect more with your close friends and family or participate in some form of group hobby. You could even add on the bonus of adding a physical activity by doing something like taking a dance class.

Even just focusing on the needs of other people can help as well. While it's important to put yourself first, sometimes it feels good to help other people out and take some of our attention away from ourselves. This is especially true when it comes to performing acts of kindness. Forming a closer connection with other people can greatly eliminate feelings of isolation (*Kindness Matters Guide*, 2022).

It can also help to bring your attention to the present moment. This is a practice often referred to as mindfulness (*5 Steps to Mental Wellbeing*, 2022).

REFLECTION

Physical and mental health are the cornerstones of taking care of yourself. Without knowing how to properly feed yourself healthy foods, exercise, and take care of your mental health, you aren't going to last very long before you make yourself unwell.

To give yourself an intimate understanding of your heart's role in physical fitness, try testing out your heart rate at rest versus when you are active. Figuring out your resting heart rate and comparing it to your heart rate after physical activity is another great way to determine your baseline for physical fitness (Mayo Clinic Staff, 2019).

It's important to make sure your heart is actually at a resting rate, so you may as well get comfy and sit down for at least five minutes before taking your pulse (Fowler, 2020). There are many different areas where you can check your pulse, but feeling for it at either your neck or your wrist is your best chance at accuracy. Your heart rate may vary, but the average resting heart rate for those aged 12-18 is around 60-100 beats per minute (BPM) (Fowler, 2020).

Figure out your resting heart rate? Excellent. Now, get up and move around! Run, do a very brisk walk, dance—anything that gets your blood pumping. Then, check your pulse again to see where your heart rate is. Compare the difference between your two heart rates.

If it is within budget, you can also consider wearing a watch designed to track your heart rate at various activity levels.

CONCLUSION

Life skills are not simply something that can help you coast through life. Rather, life skills are more like the building blocks that help you unlock your true potential. No one is born with the ability to naturally live a happy and successful life. Everyone has to work for it and develop their skills as they grow. We aren't giving you a guaranteed "this will fix your life" solution. We are simply laying the stones so you can walk the path yourself.

As we've walked down this path together, you've learned many invaluable skills. You can now manage your time by figuring out the barriers you have regarding focus, prioritizing tasks/goals, and eliminating distractions. Your study skills will have significantly improved now that you know the right and wrong ways to prepare for tests. You also know how to properly communicate, navigate the internet safely, save money, and take care of your mental and physical health.

Throughout this journey, you have learned many of the things you will need to succeed, not only in school but further on in life as well. Within you are the seeds to become anything you put your mind to. Now that you know how to manage a schedule and achieve academic success through proper communication, there are many more ways you can take these life skills even further. Maybe our chapter on physical and mental health has given you a better grasp on how you can adequately balance taking on work and school activities while ensuring that you are still looking after yourself.

Perhaps our segment on digital literacy has made you more mindful of how you use the internet, freeing your schedule even further to devote to academics or increasing your productivity in other areas of your life, such as the pursuit of hobbies. Not only that, but your newfound ability to analyze information allows you to make more decisions based on facts and critical thinking. In other words, you know the difference between someone selling you snake oil versus offering you an actual solution.

Just imagine what you'll be able to do once you leave high school behind and enter the hallowed halls of higher education. With your newly acquired study skills and a better grasp of verbal and oral communication, there is nothing stopping you from tackling any class. Maybe you'll even get on the honor society or the dean's list. In the future when you have a career, you'll know better how to interact with those surrounding you in the workplace. The possibilities of where these skills can take you are borderline infinite!

There is a misconception that once you become an adult, you're done growing. But the secret is that you never stop using and adapting your life skills. There is no best time in your life when everything just magically works out for the better. There is only right now, your choices, and the knowledge you have. Right now, you are armed with more knowledge than you were before. It's up to you where you take these skills and show us how far you can go!

GLOSSARY

401K: a company retirement plan into which employees contribute a sum of their pay

Adware: a type of computer virus that continuously shoves advertisements in your face

Aerobic: cardio exercises

Attention Deficit Hyperactivity Disorder: a mental health condition that can greatly affect concentration and the performance of certain tasks

Bankrupt: being so far in debt that you have no possible means of ever paying it back

Bonds: money that usually a company borrows from investors

Broker: a third party that acts as a go-between for a buyer and a seller

Burnout: a psychological/emotional shutdown that occurs after an extreme, long-lasting period of stress or working too hard

Cognitive Behavioral Therapy: an approach to psychological therapy

Circadian Rhythm: In simple terms, the body's sleep and wake cycle

Collateral: when taking out a loan, the lender may hold something that the borrower risks losing if they do not repay the loan

Credit: with regard to banking/finances, the expenditure of money you don't yet have with the promise of repaying the debt at a later date

Demographic: a specific subcategory of a population/group

Dialectic Behavioral Therapy: a form of mental health treatment that is generally used for those who experience emotions at an intense level

Digital Citizenship: how you behave online

Digital Footprint: anything and everything you have ever done or put on the internet

Escrow: when another party holds a sum of money until certain conditions are met; often used in real estate

Enunciate: to pronounce spoken words clearly and accurately

Ethos: ethics or moral beliefs

Eye Movement Desensitization and Reprocessing: therapy that helps patients process their feelings with controlled and deliberate eye movements

Haptics: tactile representation of nonverbal communication

Heuristics: in problem-solving, a method breaking down a problem into the most simple and easy way to solve

Hyperfocus: an extended period of attention given to a task or activity

Hypertrophy: in fitness, the continuous cycle of damaging and repairing muscles through exercise and periods of rest in order to gain strength

Investing: to put money toward something in the hope of gaining more money in return

Kinesics: the field of scientific study devoted to body language

Logos: appealing to rationality and logical thinking

Macro Nutrients: the foundation of nutritional needs, aka fats, carbs, and protein

Malware: software used to deliberately install viruses in computers, often to access sensitive/private material and disrupt the function of the software

Micronutrients: vitamins and minerals needed for optimal nutritional balance

Mnemonics: little tricks designed to help you remember certain information

Neurodivergent: the tendency to mentally think and function differently than the average person, often due to a specific set of conditions/disorders

Neurotypical: average ability to focus and function on day-to-day tasks

Paralinguistics: communication using sounds but not actual speech

Pathos: to influence through provoking emotion

Phishing Scam: when you receive a pop-up or email that tries to get you to spill private information in order to steal your identity and potentially hack your finances

Primary Source: the main source you rely on for research or essay; an example would be if you were writing a paper on Frankenstein, your primary source would be *Frankenstein*

Proxemics: the study of personal space as a form of communication

Ransomware: a virus that often follows a "pay x amount of money to get your computer working again or else" mode of attack

Secondary Source: sources outside your primary source that serve to further your argument/research

Segmentation: In psychology, the complete separation of work and play in a work-life balance

Sesquipedalian: the tendency to use long/complicated words

Social Security Number: an identifying number given to each individual in America for the purpose of tracking their finances/available financial benefits

Spyware: a virus that informs another party of the activity done in the affected computer

Stocks: when you pay into a business to own a small portion of it

Time Blindness: when you have difficulty understanding the passage of time or how much time a task requires

Trojan: a computer virus you receive when you accidentally allow it into your system often by clicking suspicious pop-ups or links

REFERENCES

"A Friend Asks" app. (n.d.). The Jason Foundation, Inc. https://jasonfoundation. com/get-involved/student/a-friend-asks-ap

Active reading strategies: Remember and analyze what you read. (n.d.). The McGraw Center for Teaching and Learning; Princeton University. https:// mcgraw.princeton.edu/undergraduates/resources/resource-library/ active-reading-strategies

Adams, R. (2022, March 17). *Start investing as a teenager + what you should invest in.* Young and the Invested. https://youngandtheinvested.com/best-invest ments-for-teenagers

ADDA Editorial Team. (2016, June 22). *The body double: A unique tool for getting things done.* ADDA. https://add.org/the-body-double

Agnafors, S., Barmark, M., & Sydsjö, G. (2020). Mental health and academic performance: A study on selection and causation effects from childhood to early adulthood. *Social Psychiatry and Psychiatric Epidemiology, 56*(5). https://doi.org/10.1007/s00127-020-01934-5.

An analysis of study habits, according to students across the U.S. (2022, March 31). Grand Canyon University. https://www.gcu.edu/blog/gcu-experience/ analysis-study-habits-according-students-across-us

Arumugam, A., Shanmugavelu, G., Yusof, F. H., Hamid, M., Manickam, M. N., Ilias, K., & Singh, J. (2021). THE IMPORTANCE OF TIME MANAGE-MENT FOR THE SUCCESS OF TEENAGERS IN EDUCATION: AN OVERVIEW. *EPRA International Journal of Multidisciplinary Research, 7*(8). : https://doi.org/10.36713/epra8291

Backstage Staff. (2022, March 3). *The best acting warmup exercises.* Backstage. https://www.backstage.com/magazine/article/vocal-physical-actor-warmup-guide-74817/#:~:text=Many%20actors%20combine%20stretch-ing%20and

Baker, M. (2023, June 15). *Youth and social media: Mental health effects, benefits, and more.* Medical News Today. https://www.medicalnewstoday.com/arti cles/youth-and-social-media#summary

Ben-Joseph, E. P. (2018, April). *Teaching kids to be smart about social media (for parents).* KidsHealth. https://kidshealth.org/en/parents/social-media-smarts.html

Bender, J. (n.d.). *How to create stronger passwords.* Business News Daily. https://www.businessnewsdaily.com/5597-create-strong-passwords.html

Birt, J. (2023, March 11). *6 ways to improve critical thinking at work.* Indeed Career Guide. https://www.indeed.com/career-advice/career-develop ment/how-to-improve-critical-thinking

Bittel, J. (2015, July 22). *Why we were totally wrong about how boa constrictors kill.* National Geographic. https://www.nationalgeographic.com/animals/arti cle/150722-boa-constrictors-snakes-animals-science-kill#:~:text=Boa%20constrictors%20were%20long%20thought

Black, R. (2017, December 31). *Glossophobia (fear of public speaking): Are you glossophobic?* PsyCom. https://www.psycom.net/glossophobia-fear-of-public-speaking

Blanton, K. (2022, March 24). *8 scientific benefits of meal prepping.* Everyday-Health. https://www.everydayhealth.com/diet-nutrition/scientific-bene fits-of-meal-prepping

Bouygues, H. L. (2019, May 6). *3 simple habits to improve your critical thinking.* Harvard Business Review. https://hbr.org/2019/05/3-simple-habits-to-improve-your-critical-thinking

Brody, B. (2021, March 7). *Slideshow: How clutter can affect your health.* WebMD. https://www.webmd.com/balance/ss/slideshow-clutter-affects-health

Brower, T. (2023, February 6). *For effective communication tone (surprise!) matters most: 5 strategies for effectiveness.* Forbes. https://www.forbes.com/sites/ tracybrower/2023/02/26/for-effective-communication-tone-surprise-matters-most-5-strategies-for-effectiveness/?sh=7d73fc5b2f9c

Butler, K. (2017, May 24). *6 myths about procrastination and productivity.* NBC News. https://www.nbcnews.com/better/careers/6-myths-you-ve-been-told-about-procrastination-productivity-n763571

Cappello, K. (2020, December 21). *The impact of sleep on learning and memory.* Perelman School of Medicine. https://www.med.upenn.edu/csi/the-impact-of-sleep-on-learning-and-memory.html

Carlton, B. (2021, September 16). *Council post: Why professionals should embrace public speaking (and how you can get started).* Forbes. https://www.forbes. com/sites/forbesbusinesscouncil/2021/09/16/why-professionals-should-

embrace-public-speaking-and-how-you-can-get-started/?sh=
25ca5558487d

Castelow, E. (2017). *A history of the town crier.* Historic UK. https://www.
historic-uk.com/CultureUK/The-Town-Crier

Chen, J. (2003, November 21). *Debt: What it is, how it works, types, and ways to
pay back.* Investopedia. https://www.investopedia.com/terms/d/debt.
asp#:~:

Chen, J. (2022, September 21). *Heuristics.* Investopedia. https://www.investo
pedia.com/terms/h/heuristics.asp

Cherry, K. (2023, February 22). *Types of nonverbal communication.* Verywell
Mind. https://www.verywellmind.com/types-of-nonverbal-communica
tion-2795397

Clarke, J. (2019). *How empathy can improve your relationships.* Verywell Mind.
https://www.verywellmind.com/cognitive-and-emotional-empathy-
4582389

Clifford, E. (2017, May 29). *16 young and successful entrepreneurs who prove that
age is nothing but a number.* Lifehack. https://www.lifehack.org/588440/
16-young-and-successful-entrepreneurs-who-prove-that-age-is-nothing-
but-a-number

Consky, M. (2023, March 26). *Taking breaks at work? New study shows they boost
your productivity.* CTVNews. https://www.ctvnews.ca/business/taking-
breaks-at-work-new-study-shows-they-boost-your-productivity-1.
6329580

Cooks-Campbell, A. (2022, October 28). *15+ self-care tips for mental health:
Strategies, tips, and resources.* BetterUp. https://www.betterup.com/blog/
self-care-tips-for-mental-health

Coombes, A. (2021, December 16). *What is a Roth IRA?* Forbes Advisor.
https://www.forbes.com/advisor/retirement/roth-ira

Cote, C. (2021, January 7). *How to improve your analytical skills.* Business
Insights. https://online.hbs.edu/blog/post/how-to-improve-analytical-
skills

Critical reading techniques. (2018). The Open University. https://help.open.ac.
uk/active-reading

Cuncic, A. (2021, May 28). *6 ways to improve your body language skills.* Verywell
Mind. https://www.verywellmind.com/an-overview-of-body-language-
3024872

Cuncic, A. (2022, November 9). *What is active listening?* Verywell Mind. https://www.verywellmind.com/what-is-active-listening-3024343

Cyberbullying: What is it and how to stop it. (n.d.). UNICEF. https://www.unicef.org/end-violence/how-to-stop-cyberbullying#2

Davidson, K. (2020, December 3). *5 tips for developing a better relationship with food.* Healthline. https://www.healthline.com/nutrition/fixing-a-bad-relationship-with-food

Davydenko, M., Kolbuszewska, M., & Peetz, J. (2021). A meta-analysis of financial self-control strategies: Comparing empirical findings with online media and lay person perspectives on what helps individuals curb spending and start saving. *PLOS ONE, 16*(7), e0253938. https://doi.org/10.1371/journal.pone.0253938

Deutsch, A. (2019). *Watch out for these top internet scams.* Investopedia. https://www.investopedia.com/articles/personal-finance/040115/watch-out-these-top-internet-scams.asp

Digital footprint. (2022, January 12). Canadian Centre for Cyber Security. https://www.cyber.gc.ca/en/guidance/digital-footprint-itsap00133

Eaton, S. E. (2011, July 12). *21 photos you should never post on social media.* Learning, Teaching and Leadership. https://drsaraheaton.wordpress.com/2011/07/12/photos-you-should-not-share-on-social-media

Edgar, L. (2022, October 4). *The importance of enunciation.* Decoda Literacy Solutions. https://decoda.ca/the-importance-of-enunciation

Editing vs. proofreading: Know the difference. (n.d.). Editage. https://www.editage.com/all-about-publication/english-editing/editing-proofreading

Emihovich, B., Roque, N., & Mason, J. (2020). Can video gameplay improve undergraduates' problem-solving skills? *International Journal of Game-Based Learning, 10*(2), 21–38. https://doi.org/10.4018/ijgbl.2020040102

Ernst, A., Bertrand, J. M. F., Voltzenlogel, V., Souchay, C., & Moulin, C. J. A. (2021). The Proust Machine: What a public science event tells us about autobiographical memory and the five senses. *Frontiers in Psychology, 11.* https://doi.org/10.3389/fpsyg.2020.623910

Farhud, D. D. (2015). Impact of lifestyle on health. *Iranian Journal of Public Health, 44*(11), 1442–1444. https://www.ncbi.nlm.nih.gov/pmc/articles/PMC4703222/#B1

Filestage. (2018, August 21). *11 proven methods for meeting deadlines.* The Project Success Blog. https://filestage.io/blog/meeting-deadlines

51 critical cyber bullying statistics in 2019. (2022). Broadband Search. https://www.broadbandsearch.net/blog/cyber-bullying-statistics

5 steps to mental wellbeing. (2022, December 16). NHS. https://www.nhs.uk/mental-health/self-help/guides-tools-and-activities/five-steps-to-mental-wellbeing

5 quick tips for navigating the internet like a pro. (2017, November 29). English Online Live&Learn. https://livelearn.ca/article/digital-citizenship/5-quick-tips-for-navigating-the-internet-like-a-pro

Fontinelle, A. (2021, March 29). *Setting financial goals for your future.* Investopedia. https://www.investopedia.com/articles/personal-finance/100516/setting-financial-goals

Food for teenagers: Meal plan on the cheap! (2021, January 18). Shelf Cooking. https://shelfcooking.com/food-for-teenagers

Fowler, P. (2020, August 25). *Children's vital signs: what do the numbers tell you?* WebMD. https://www.webmd.com/children/children-vital-signs

Ganti, A. (2023, April 30). *Budget definition.* Investopedia. https://www.investopedia.com/terms/b/budget.asp

Goal-setting. (2023). CALE Learning Enhancement, Eastern Washington University. https://inside.ewu.edu/calelearning/psychological-skills/goal-setting

Got stage fright? Try these 14 effective tricks to calm your nerves. (2022, September 2). Forbes. https://www.forbes.com/sites/forbescoachescouncil/2022/09/22/got-stage-fright-try-these-14-effective-tricks-to-calm-your-nerves/?sh=d95adb6c3d0c

Griffin, T. (2021, September 15). *Council post: Three ways to use time blocking for better time management.* Forbes. https://www.forbes.com/sites/theyec/2021/09/15/three-ways-to-use-time-blocking-for-better-time-management/?sh=5f78fc9437f9

Grossel, S. (2020, October 6). *Your guide to being a good digital citizen.* Temple University. https://news.temple.edu/nutshell/2020-10-06/digital-citizenship-0

Guidelines for creating a study schedule. (n.d.). Cornell University. https://lsc.cornell.edu/how-to-study/studying-for-and-taking-exams/guidelines-for-creating-a-study-schedule

Guides: Study effectively: The Cornell Method of note-taking. (2017, September 11). University of Guelph. https://guides.lib.uoguelph.ca/StudyEffectively/CornellMethod

Harper, J. (2023, June 7). *18 tips for meeting deadlines.* Indeed Career Guide. https://www.indeed.com/career-advice/career-development/meet-the-deadline

Highlighting. (2016). University of North Carolina at Chapel Hill. https://learningcenter.unc.edu/tips-and-tools/using-highlighters

Hoffses, K. (2018). *Test anxiety (for teens).* KidsHealth. https://kidshealth.org/en/teens/test-anxiety.html

How logical reasoning works. (n.d.). BrainGymmer. https://www.braingymmer.com/en/blog/logical-reasoning

How to avoid sharing too much information online. (2021, September 7). Government of Canada. https://www.getcybersafe.gc.ca/en/blogs/how-avoid-sharing-too-much-information-online

How to create a study space. (2020, June 10). Maryville University. https://online.maryville.edu/blog/how-to-create-a-study-space/

How to evaluate anti-virus software (and choose the right one for you). (2020, August 12). Government of Canada. https://www.getcybersafe.gc.ca/en/blogs/how-evaluate-anti-virus-software-and-choose-right-one-you

How to identify and protect yourself from an unsafe website. (n.d.). BU TechWeb. https://www.bu.edu/tech/support/information-security/security-for-everyone/how-to-identify-and-protect-yourself-from-an-unsafe-website/#:

How to identify reliable information online. (2023). Stevenson University. https://www.stevenson.edu/online/about-us/news/how-to-identify-reliable-information/

How to improve your presentation skills. (2022, November 25). University of Sheffield. https://usic.sheffield.ac.uk/blog/how-to-improve-your-presentation-skills

How to make an effective study plan. (n.d.). Victoria University, Australia. https://www.vu.edu.au/about-vu/news-events/study-space/how-to-make-an-effective-study-plan

How to recognize and avoid phishing scams. (2019, May 3). Federal Trade Commission. https://consumer.ftc.gov/articles/how-recognize-and-avoid-phishing-scams

Hubbard, A. (2020, September 11). *6 reasons why working from bed isn't a good idea.* Healthline. https://www.healthline.com/health/working-from-bed-isnt-doing-you-favors

Improving your credit score. (2016, May 27). Government of Canada. https://www.canada.ca/en/financial-consumer-agency/services/credit-reports-score/improve-credit-score.html

Indeed Editorial Team. (2021, February 10). *10 ways to improve your analytical skills.* Indeed Career Guide. https://www.indeed.com/career-advice/career-development/improve-analytical-skills

Indeed Editorial Team. (2023a, April 12). *Everything you need to know about written communication.* Indeed Career Guide. https://www.indeed.com/career-advice/career-development/written-communication

Indeed Editorial Team. (2023b, April 28). *Problem-solving skills: Definitions and examples.* Indeed Career Guide. https://ca.indeed.com/career-advice/career-development/problem-solving-skills

International Association for Suicide Prevention. (2013). *International Association for Suicide Prevention.* https://www.iasp.info

Internet safety for kids: Staying safe from online predators. (2019). Goodwill Community Foundation. https://edu.gcfglobal.org/en/internetsafetyforkids/staying-safe-from-online-predators/1/

Jenkins, P. (2022, April 13). *Why doesn't school teach life skills?* Brillantio. https://brilliantio.com/why-doesnt-school-teach-life-skills/#:~:

Kagan, J. (2019a). *Loan shark definition.* Investopedia. https://www.investopedia.com/terms/l/loansharking.asp

Kagan, J. (2019b, April 19). *Loan definition.* Investopedia. https://www.investopedia.com/terms/l/loan.asp

Kaspersky. (2021, June 4). *How to identify fake news.* Kaspersky. https://www.kaspersky.com/resource-center/preemptive-safety/how-to-identify-fake-news

Kindness matters guide. (2022). Mental Health Foundation. https://www.mentalhealth.org.uk/explore-mental-health/kindness/kindness-matters-guide

Knueven, L. (2022, December 9). *How to save money as a teenager so you can get yourself a car, pay for college, or take a trip.* Business Insider. https://www.businessinsider.com/personal-finance/how-to-save-money-as-a-teenager

Lake, R. (2022, January 2). *Want a better credit score? Here's how to get it.* Investopedia. https://www.investopedia.com/how-to-improve-your-credit-score-4590097

Lancaster, M. R., & Callaghan, P. (2022). The effect of exercise on resilience, its mediators and moderators, in a general population during the UK

COVID-19 pandemic in 2020: a cross-sectional online study. *BMC Public Health*, *22*(1). https://doi.org/10.1186/s12889-022-13070-7

Lane, C. (2020, January). *Does cramming for your exams actually work?* Top Universities. https://www.topuniversities.com/blog/does-cramming-your-exams-actually-work

Lehmann, J. A. M., & Seufert, T. (2017). The Influence of background music on learning in the light of different theoretical perspectives and the role of working memory capacity. *Frontiers in Psychology*, *8*(1902). https://doi.org/10.3389/fpsyg.2017.01902

Liberto, D. (2023, March 1). *Stock market for teens*. Investopedia. https://www.investopedia.com/stock-market-for-teens-7112213#:~:text=You%20usu-ally%20need%20to%20be

Life skills education for children and adolescents in schools. (1994). *World Health Organization. Division of Mental Health.* https://apps.who.int/iris/handle/10665/63552

Lillico, H. G., Hammond, D., Manske, S., & Murnaghan, D. (2014). The prevalence of eating behaviors among Canadian youth using cross-sectional school-based surveys. *BMC Public Health*, *14*(1). https://doi.org/10.1186/1471-2458-14-323

Locke, E. A., & Latham, G. P. (2002). Building a practically useful theory of goal setting and task motivation: A 35-year odyssey. *American Psychologist*, *57*(9), 705–717.

Lovering, N. (2022, June 24). *8 evidence-based study habits: What research says works*. Psych Central. https://psychcentral.com/health/highly-effective-study-habits#positive-study-habits

Mandal, A. (2020, May). *The Pomodoro Technique: An effective time management tool*. NICHD. https://science.nichd.nih.gov/confluence/display/newsletter/2020/05/07/The+Pomodoro+Technique%3A+An+Effective+Time+Management+Tool

Martinovich, M. (2017, May 5). *Studying more strategically equals improved exam scores*. Stanford University. https://news.stanford.edu/2017/05/08/studying-strategically-equals-improved-exam-scores

Mayo Clinic Staff. (2018). *10 great reasons to love aerobic exercise*. Mayo Clinic. https://www.mayoclinic.org/healthy-lifestyle/fitness/in-depth/aerobic-exercise/art-20045541

Mayo Clinic Staff. (2019). *5 steps to start a fitness program*. Mayo Clinic. https://www.mayoclinic.org/healthy-lifestyle/fitness/in-depth/fitness/art-

20048269

Mayo Clinic Staff. (2022a, February 26). *How to help your teen navigate social media*. Mayo Clinic. https://www.mayoclinic.org/healthy-lifestyle/tween-and-teen-health/in-depth/teens-and-social-media-use/art-20474437?reDate=13092023

Mayo Clinic Staff. (2022b, August 3). *Exercise and stress: Get moving to manage stress*. Mayo Clinic. https://www.mayoclinic.org/healthy-lifestyle/stress-management/in-depth/exercise-and-stress/art-20044469#:~

Medojevic, L. (2022, January 31). *Six top tips for writing a great essay*. University of Melbourne. https://students.unimelb.edu.au/academic-skills/resources/essay-writing/six-top-tips-for-writing-a-great-essay

Mental health of adolescents. (2021). World Health Organization. https://www.who.int/news-room/fact-sheets/detail/adolescent-mental-health

MindTools Content Team. (n.d.). *Effective Scheduling*. MindTools. https://www.mindtools.com/ak2ljl6/effective-scheduling

MindTools Content Team. (2023). *Brainstorming*. MindTools. https://www.mindtools.com/acv0de1/brainstorming

Moffatt, C. (n.d.). *All guides: Taking notes module: Charting Method*. Sheridan Library and Learning Services. https://sheridancollege.libguides.com/takingnotesmodule/taking-notes-in-class/charting-method#:~

Momma, H., Kawakami, R., Honda, T., & Sawada, S. S. (2022). Muscle-strengthening activities are associated with lower risk and mortality in major non-communicable diseases: a systematic review and meta-analysis of cohort studies. *British Journal of Sports Medicine, 56*(13). https://doi.org/10.1136/bjsports-2021-105061

Mrazek, A. J., Mrazek, M. D., Ortega, J. R., Ji, R. R., Karimi, S. S., Brown, C. S., Alexander, C. A., Khan, M., Panahi, R., Sadoff, M., Scott, A., Tyszka, J. E., & Schooler, J. W. (2021). Teenagers' smartphone use during homework: An analysis of beliefs and behaviors around digital multitasking. *Education Sciences, 11*(11), 713. https://doi.org/10.3390/educsci11110713

Muntingh, L. (2021, September 30). *18 internet safety statistics for 2022*. Screen and Reveal. https://screenandreveal.com/internet-safety-statistics/#google_vignette

Muscad, O. (2022, August 29). *The comprehensive guide to the 5W1H Method*. DATAMYTE. https://datamyte.com/5w1h-method-comprehensive-guide/#:~

Nash, J. (2018, January 5). *How to set healthy boundaries & build positive relation-*

ships. Positive Psychology. https://positivepsychology.com/great-self-care-setting-healthy-boundaries/#healthy

Nelson, J. B. (2017). Mindful eating: The art of presence while you eat. *Diabetes Spectrum, 30*(3), 171–174. https://doi.org/10.2337/ds17-0015

Nine signs of mental health issues. (2019, February 12). Health Direct. https://www.healthdirect.gov.au/signs-mental-health-issue

Nortje, A. (2021, March 17). *Work-life balance in psychology: 12 examples and theories*. Positive Psychology. https://positivepsychology.com/what-is-work-life-balance/#google_vignette

Nutrition. (2022). World Health Organization. https://www.who.int/health-topics/nutrition#tab=tab_1

Online disinformation. (2023, February 7). Government of Canada. https://www.canada.ca/en/campaign/online-disinformation.html

O'Shea, C. (2023, August). *Test-taking tips (for teens)*. KidsHealth. https://kidshealth.org/en/teens/testing-tips.html

Opening a bank account. (2017, January 10). Government of Canada. https://www.canada.ca/en/financial-consumer-agency/services/banking/opening-bank-account.html

Oshin, M. (2018, May 1). *Elon Musk's "time blocking" method: How to manage time effectively even if your schedule is hectic*. Mayo Oshin. https://www.mayooshin.com/time-blocking-elon-musk-manage-time

Parkhurst, E. (2021, October 25). *How hobbies improve mental health*. Utah State University. https://extension.usu.edu/mentalhealth/articles/how-hobbies-improve-mental-health

Pathos, logos, and ethos. (2021). STLCC. https://stlcc.edu/student-support/academic-success-and-tutoring/writing-center/writing-resources/pathos-logos-and-ethos.aspx

Paul, N. P., Galván, A. E., Yoshinaga-Sakurai, K., Rosen, B. P., & Yoshinaga, M. (2022). Arsenic in medicine: Past, present and future. *BioMetals*. https://doi.org/10.1007/s10534-022-00371-y

Pedersen, T. (2016, May 17). *Memory and mnemonic devices*. Psych Central. https://psychcentral.com/lib/memory-and-mnemonic-devices

Pedersen, T. (2022, March 31). *Mnemonic devices: Types, examples, and benefits*. Psych Central. https://psychcentral.com/lib/memory-and-mnemonic-devices#examples

Pfleegor, K. (2021, July 21). *Research guides: Reading and study strategies: Anno-*

tating a text. Eastern Washington University. https://research.ewu.edu/writers_c_read_study_strategies

Physical activity facts. (2020, April 21). Centers for Disease Control and Prevention. https://www.cdc.gov/healthyschools/physicalactivity/facts.htm#:~:

Picardo, E. (2022, July 22). *Investing definition*. Investopedia. https://www.investopedia.com/terms/i/investing.asp

Piontec, N. (2020, November 5). *10 ways to improve your English vocabulary*. Grammarly. https://www.grammarly.com/blog/how-to-improve-english

Pombo, E. (2019, February 1). *Self-help techniques for coping with mental illness*. NAMI. https://www.nami.org/Blogs/NAMI-Blog/January-2019/Self-Help-Techniques-for-Coping-with-Mental-Illness

Prajapati, R., Sharma, B., & Sharma, D. (2017). Significance of life skills education. *Contemporary Issues in Education Research (CIER), 10*(1), 1–6. https://doi.org/10.19030/cier.v10i1.9875

Research guides: How to evaluate information sources: Identify bias. (2019). New Jersey Institute of Technology. https://researchguides.njit.edu/evaluate/bias

Richmond, S. (2021, April 12). Key life skills adults wish they'd been taught at school. *The Independent*. https://www.independent.co.uk/news/education/parents-schools-life-skills-survey-b1830010.html

Rosenkrantz, H. (2022, December 15). *Strategies for increased reading comprehension*. U.S. News. https://www.usnews.com/education/k12/articles/strategies-to-increase-reading-comprehension

Ryder, G. (2021, October 21). *How to understand and read body language*. Psych Central. https://psychcentral.com/health/body-language#understanding-and-reading-it

Schmaltz, R. M., Jansen, E., & Wenckowski, N. (2017). Redefining critical thinking: Teaching students to think like scientists. *Frontiers in Psychology, 8*. https://doi.org/10.3389/fpsyg.2017.00459

Scott, E. (2020, November 24). *The importance of self-care for health and stress management*. Verywell Mind. https://www.verywellmind.com/importance-of-self-care-for-health-stress-management-3144704

Self-care: 5 ways to take good care of yourself. (2021, December 21). Geisinger. https://www.geisinger.org/health-and-wellness/wellness-articles/2021/01/11/16/10/5-self-care-tips#:~

Seven effective ways to proofread writing. (n.d.). Touro College. https://www.

touro.edu/departments/writing-center/tutorials/seven-steps-to-effec tive-proofreading/

Shishegar, N., & Boubekri, M. (2016). Natural light and productivity: Analyzing the impacts of daylighting on students' and workers' health and alertness. *International Journal of Advances in Chemical Engineering and Biological Sciences, 3*(1). https://doi.org/10.15242/ijacebs.ae0416104

SickKids Staff. (2019). *Healthy eating for teens.* About Kids Health. https:// www.aboutkidshealth.ca/Article?contentid=638&language=English

Sleep and Health. (2019, September 11). Centers for Disease Control and Prevention. https://www.cdc.gov/healthyschools/sleep.htm#:~:

Smith, A. (2020, June 30). *Types of therapy: For anxiety, depression, trauma, PTSD and more.* Medical News Today. https://www.medicalnewstoday.com/arti cles/types-of-therapy

Smith, K. A., & Underwood, J. (2023, May 1). *What is the 50/30/20 rule?* Forbes. https://www.forbes.com/advisor/banking/guide-to-50-30-20- budget/#:~:

Spence, J. (2020, February 18). *Nonverbal communication: How body language & nonverbal cues are key.* Lifesize. https://www.lifesize.com/blog/speaking- without-words/#:~:

Spencer, S. (2022, February 18). *"Fake news" & misinformation: How to fact check.* University of Tampa. https://utopia.ut.edu/FakeNews/factcheck

Stouffer, C. (2021, August 27). *10 types of malware + how to prevent malware from the start.* Norton. https://us.norton.com/blog/malware/types-of-malware

Suicide prevention resources. (2023, January 12). Centers for Disease Control and Prevention. https://www.cdc.gov/suicide/resources/

Tartakovsky, M. (2015, July 8). *9 tips for identifying and living your priorities.* Psych Central. https://psychcentral.com/blog/9-tips-for-identifying-and- living-your-priorities#6

Tavel, R. (2023, January 4). *How to build muscle, according to experts.* Forbes Health. https://www.forbes.com/health/fitness/how-to-build-muscle/

10 tips for planning meals on a budget. (n.d.). Unlock Food. https://www.unlock food.ca/en/Articles/Budget/10-Tips-for-Planning-Meals-on-a-Budget

Thalluri, J. (2016). Who benefits most from peer support group? First year student success for pathology students. *Procedia - Social and Behavioral Sciences, 228*, 39–44. https://doi.org/10.1016/j.sbspro.2016.07.006

The 7 benefits of effective communication in personal and professional settings. (2019, July 9). Portland Community College. https://climb.pcc.edu/blog/

the-7-benefits-of-effective-communication-in-personal-and-profes
sional-settings

The benefits of critical thinking for students. (2021, April 1). Thadomal Shahani Centre for Management. https://tscfm.org/blogs/the-benefits-of-critical-thinking-for-students/

The Investopedia Team. (2020). *Credit: What everyone should know.* Investopedia. https://www.investopedia.com/terms/c/credit.asp

The real reason you're procrastinating. (2022, September 28). McLean Hospital. https://www.mcleanhospital.org/essential/procrastination

Tips for effective proofreading. (2009, November 11). UA Little Rock. https://ualr.edu/writingcenter/tips-for-effective-proofreading

Trepany, C. (2023, July 21). *A TikToker went viral for blaming being late to work on "time blindness." Is it a real thing?* USA TODAY. https://www.usatoday.com/story/life/health-wellness/2023/07/21/time-blindness-viral-tiktok-is-it-real-adhd-symptom/70440407007

Tretina, K. (2023, September 1). *Best investment accounts for kids.* Forbes. https://www.forbes.com/advisor/investing/best-investment-accounts-for-kids/

Turner, T. (2023, February 3). *47+ fascinating financial literacy statistics in 2022.* Annuity. https://www.annuity.org/financial-literacy/financial-literacy-statistics/

Van Edwards, V. (2013, September 6). *The definitive guide to reading.* Science of People. https://www.scienceofpeople.com/microexpressions/

VanSonnenberg, E. (2011, January 3). *Ready, set, goals!* Positive Psychology News. https://positivepsychologynews.com/news/emily-vansonnenberg/2011010315821

Warning signs. (n.d.). The Jason Foundation. https://jasonfoundation.com/youth-suicide/warning-signs

Waters, S. (2022, March 8). *Problem-solving strategies: How to turn challenges into opportunities.* BetterUp. https://www.betterup.com/blog/problem-solving-strategies

Watson, A. (2022, July 15). *Journalists seeing fake information U.S. 2022.* Statista. https://www.statista.com/statistics/1319457/journalists-finding-false-information-us

Watson, A. (2023, May 11). *Accuracy of news on social media 2018.* Statista. https://www.statista.com/statistics/875065/social-media-accuracy-perceptions

Williams, G. (2023, February 28). *Is fast food cheaper than cooking at home?* U.S. News.   https://money.usnews.com/money/personal-finance/articles/is-fast-food-cheaper-than-cooking-at-home

Yusefzadeh, H., Amirzadeh Iranagh, J., & Nabilou, B. (2019). The effect of study preparation on test anxiety and performance: a quasi-experimental study. *Advances in Medical Education and Practice, Volume 10,* 245–251. https://doi.org/10.2147/amep.s192053